Seniors' Rights

Your Legal Guide to Living Life to the Fullest

Other books in the *Rights* series:

Attorney Responsibilities and Client Rights
by Susan Herskowitz Singer

Employees' Rights
by Richard C. Busse

Employer's Rights
by Charles H. Fleischer

Gay & Lesbian Rights
by Brette McWhorter Sember

Homeowner's Rights
by Mark Warda

Teen Rights
by Traci Truly

Traveler's Rights
by Alexander Anolik and John K. Hawks

Unmarried Parents' Rights, 2nd Ed.
by Jacqueline D. Stanley

Seniors' Rights

You Legal Guide to Living Life to the Fullest

Brette McWhorter Sember

Attorney at Law

SPHINX® PUBLISHING
AN IMPRINT OF SOURCEBOOKS, INC.®
NAPERVILLE, ILLINOIS
www.SphinxLegal.com

First Edition: 2004

Published by: **Sphinx® Publishing, An Imprint of Sourcebooks, Inc.®**

Naperville Office
P. O. Box 4410
Naperville, Illinois 60567-4410
630-961-3900
Fax: 630-961-2168
www.sourcebooks.com
www.SphinxLegal.com

This publication is designed to provide accurate and authoritative information in regard to the subject matter covered. It is sold with the understanding that the publisher is not engaged in rendering legal, accounting, or other professional service. If legal advice or other expert assistance is required, the services of a competent professional person should be sought.

From a Declaration of Principles Jointly Adopted by a Committee of t
he American Bar Association and a Committee of Publishers and Associations

This product is not a substitute for legal advice.

Disclaimer required by Texas statutes.

Library of Congress Cataloging-in-Publication Data

Sember, Brette McWhorter, 1968-
Seniors' rights : your legal guide to living life to the fullest / by Brette McWhorter Sember.-- 1st ed.
p. cm.
Includes index.
ISBN 1-57248-386-5 (alk. paper)
1. Aged--Legal status, laws, etc.--United States--Popular works. 2. Aged--Civil rights--United States--Popular works. 3. Retirees--Legal status, laws, etc.--United States--Popular works. 4. Retirees--Civil rights--United States--Popular works. I. Title.
KF390.A4S45 2004
342.7308'774--dc22

2004010704

Printed and bound in the United States of America.

BG — 10 9 8 7 6 5 4 3 2 1

CONTENTS

INTRODUCTION

They are not called the *golden years* for nothing you know! As a senior, you probably have an active, full, and satisfying life filled with friends, family, activities, and maybe a job you love. This time of your life is a wonderful period. This book is designed to help you make the most of these years.

Being a senior brings with it many concerns and special issues. You may start thinking about affording medical care, making the most of your benefits, and making sure you are treated fairly in all aspects of your life. This book will help you understand your rights about medical care, bank accounts, retirement accounts, housing, discrimination, grandchildren, and more.

Chapter 1 discusses financial matters such as applying for and receiving benefits and pensions, as well as bank accounts and investments. Chapter 2 will help you understand the health insurance and prescription program options available to you and explain how to become eligible and apply, as well as deal with any problems. Choosing health care providers and understanding your rights while receiving medical care is the subject of Chapter 3.

Chapter 4 offers information about lifestyle assistance and benefits that you may be able to access. Where you live is one of the most important parts of life and Chapter 5 examines the various options, including nursing homes, senior living, assisted living, continuing care communities, remaining at home, and more.

Chapter 6 addresses safety and ways to deal with and protect yourself from nursing home problems, elder abuse, scams and home dangers.

Your family is probably the most important part of your life, but sometimes issues do arise causing family problems. Chapter 7 will help you understand your rights and options when dealing with or considering divorce, grandparent's visitation rights, raising grandchildren yourself, remarriage, roommates, stepfamilies, and more. Chapter 8 will help you make decisions about wills and health care directives as you plan for the future. Although you hope to never lose your spouse, Chapter 9 helps you think about some of the issues and problems that you might face should this happen and offers you solutions and information should it ever happen.

Discrimination based on age or disability is a great concern for many seniors and Chapter 10 explains what your rights are and how to solve any problems that might come up. This chapter also discusses the rights of the disabled. Veteran's benefits are an important right for many people and Chapter 11 discusses how to access them. Obtaining affordable legal assistance can be difficult and Chapter 12 explains how to find free or reduced fee legal help, as well as how to find and work with an attorney, whether you pay him or her or not.

–1–

FINANCES

Dealing with finances is probably one of the most important aspects of your life, whether you are currently retired or planning for retirement. Managing retirement accounts, Social Security, pensions, and medical costs today, along with planning for the future, can all be difficult and confusing.

THINKING ABOUT THE FUTURE

While you are probably in complete control of your financial life at this stage, you have to realize that at some future date you may need some help. That help will probably come from a family member. Take the time now to organize your records, files, and information so that should you need someone to help you with it in the future, it will be easier to navigate.

Keep all important documents in a fireproof file cabinet, safe-deposit box, or in-home safe. The documents that should be kept in one of these items include:

- wills;
- powers of attorney;
- stock certificates;
- investment and pension information;
- insurance policies;
- Social Security cards;

- deeds and titles to homes and vehicles;
- bonds; and,
- cash.

Make sure other people in your family know the whereabouts of your documents and how to access them. Use the *Basic Information Organization Sheet* from Appendix G to gather all of your important information into one place so that if anyone needs to access it, it will all be together.

Powers of Attorney

Think about asking your attorney to draw up a *power of attorney* for you to sign, giving authority to someone else to manage your affairs should you become unable to at some point in the future. (See Chapter 8 for more information.)

Financial Planning

An important part of managing the financial aspects of your life is working with a trusted financial planner. A good financial planner can help you plan for retirement, explain when you can withdraw from certain accounts, and make sure that your savings continue to support you. You may also wish to work with an attorney who is experienced in Medicaid planning. Chapter 2 discusses how you qualify for Medicaid, but there are things you can do now that can protect your assets, such as transfers and trusts. (See Chapter 2 for more information about Medicaid planning.)

SOCIAL SECURITY

To qualify for Social Security benefits, you must have worked a certain number of years. Your eligibility is measured in credits. If you were born after 1929, you must accumulate forty credits or work for ten years to qualify. You earn one credit for each quarter of the year you work.

You can begin to receive benefits as early as age 62, but you will need to carefully weigh this decision—up to a certain point, the longer you wait to receive benefits, the higher your payments will be once you begin to receive them. When you do decide you want to start receiving benefits, you should contact your local Social Security office and ask them which month is best for you to begin receiving benefits. Depending on which month you begin, you may get a higher payment because you may have earned an additional work credit. Full retirement age is 65 for those born before 1938 and up to age 67 for those born after 1960.

SENIOR TIP

To apply for Social Security benefits, you can use the online form at:

www.ssa.gov/online/forms.html

or call 800-772-1213.

If your spouse is receiving benefits and you are over age 62, you may be eligible to receive benefits as well. The amount is about half of what the spouse receives.

To apply for benefits, you will need the following documents:

- your birth certificate;
- your social security number;
- military discharge papers if you were in the service;
- your spouse's birth certificate and Social Security number if he or she is also applying; and,
- your bank account number and name of your bank, so payments can be deposited.

When you apply, you must either bring original documents or send certified copies. You can find out what your monthly benefit amount would be through a yearly summary explaining your benefits. You can sign up to receive this summary automatically by mail each year. Check with your local office for sign-up information

SENIOR TIP

Your Social Security benefits are based on your average earnings during your life. To calculate your benefits, use the online calculators at:

www.ssa.gov/planners/calculators.htm

listed in the government pages of your phone book or online at **www.ssa.gov**.

Divorce

A divorced spouse can receive payments based on the former spouse if the marriage lasted at least ten years. You can begin to receive benefits when you are age 62, but only if you have not remarried. You may get benefits even if your former spouse has not yet retired if you have been divorced for at least two years, but your former spouse must have enough credits to retire.

Changes

When you are receiving benefits, you have the responsibility to notify Social Security of certain changes, including:

- address or phone number;
- bank account;
- amount of earned income;
- if you become unable to manage funds (Social Security has a program called *representative payee* in which your benefits are sent to the relative or friend who is managing your funds for you);
- if you begin to receive a pension;
- if you get married;
- if you get divorced;
- if you change your name; or,
- if you travel for a long period of time to another country.

Appeals

It is important to remember that you have the right to appeal all decisions made by Social Security. You can read about the appeals process at **www.ssa.gov/pubs/10041.html**. You have the right to be represented by an attorney at any stage in the process.

> **SENIOR TIP**
>
> You can report these changes online at:
>
> **https://s044a90.ssa.gov/apps6/ICOA/coa001.jsp**

The appeals process has four stages.

Step 1: Reconsideration. You have sixty days to submit a form (which your local representative will help you complete) asking that your benefits be reconsidered. If you were already receiving benefits and benefits are denied, you have ten days.

Step 2: Administrative hearing. If you are not happy with the results of the reconsideration, you have sixty days from the date you received denial of the reconsideration to apply to have your case heard by an administrative law judge.

Step 3: Appeals Council. You have sixty days from the date you receive the ALJ determination to appeal to the Appeals Council.

Step 4: Federal Court. If the Appeals Council will not take your case, you can appeal to a federal court and you will need an attorney to do so.

If you should win an appeal, you will be entitled to receive any lost benefits from the date of denial.

Overpayments

Overpayments are unfortunately a problem that does happen. If the Social Security Administration makes a mistake and pays you more than you are entitled to, you do have to pay it back, or it will be withheld from a future payment. You have the right to appeal an overpayment mistake. Go to your local office and tell them you want to request reconsideration of the overpayment.

Representative Payee

Should you ever become unable to manage your own affairs, Social Security can appoint someone else to be in charge of handling your payments on your behalf. This can be a family member, friend, or even a nursing home. If one is appointed for you, you must be notified in writing first. You can challenge this by an appeal (contact your local office for details).

RETIREMENT BENEFITS

You are eligible for your employer's pension plan if you have worked there for one year and at least 1000 hours. Employers offer two basic types of retirement accounts—*defined contribution plans* or *defined benefit plans*.

Defined contribution plans are characterized by an annual contribution being made for each employee. The contribution can be up to 15% of the amount the employee puts into the plan. The benefit you receive is the *vested* amount (amount that you fully own—some plans have a gradual vesting approach) plus investment income. Examples of this kind of plan are 401(k)s, 403(b) plans, employee stock ownership plans, profit-sharing plans, and money-purchase pension plans (in which the employer must contribute a specific amount each year). You will ultimately receive the balance in your account, which is based on contributions plus or minus investment gains or losses. The value of your account will fluctuate due to changes in the value of your investments.

Defined benefit plans are characterized by employer contributions that are determined by actuarial tables based on your salary and years of employment. This plan offers a monthly benefit once you retire and is considered a traditional retirement plan.

Specific kinds of retirement accounts you might have include the following.

- *Simplified Employee Pension Plan* (SEP)—the employee sets up an *Individual Retirement Plan* (IRA) and the employer makes contributions to it (up to 15 % of your pay).
- 401(k)—the employee defers receiving part of his or her salary, which is then placed in the account of payment and is untaxed at the time.

Pension and retirement plans are governed by the federal law, *Employee Retirement Income Security Act* (ERISA). Each year you must be given the plan's summary annual report which will show you how the money is being invested and the type of return on it.

To be able to receive your retirement benefits, you must become *vested*, which means you must have worked the required number of years or hours to obtain ownership of your money in the plan. Once you are vested, the funds in the account are yours, even if you leave before reaching the full retirement age.

Vesting is a gradual process. For example, after working three years you may become 20% vested, meaning that 20% of the funds in the account will be yours. It usually takes five to seven years to become completely vested. If you leave your job before you are fully vested, you lose that portion that is not yet vested. A *break in service*—time period where you temporarily leave your job—can cancel pension credits earned before you leave. Each plan is different and you need to determine the rules under your plan

You must start to be paid from the account within sixty days of turning 65 or, if earlier, the normal retirement age for your plan; the end of the 10th year after you began participation in the plan; or, you leave your job, whichever happens last.

Receiving Benefits

To receive benefits, you must first file a claim, which is simply a form saying you want to begin to receive payment. Information about how to do this must be included in the summary plan description, which you are entitled to receive within thirty days of requesting it. You are also entitled to receive a statement of your personal benefit account, which explains what is in your account and how vested you are. If, for any reason, information about the filing of a claim has not been provided, you may give notice that you have a claim by writing to an officer of your employer, the unit where claims are normally filed, or the plan administrator.

Within ninety days after you have filed a claim for benefits, your plan must tell you whether or not you will receive the benefits. If your claim is denied, the plan administrator must notify you in writing and explain in detail why it was denied. If you receive no answer after ninety days—or 180 days if an extension of time was needed—the claim is considered a denial and you can use the plan's rules for appealing the denial.

ERISA guarantees that pension rights cannot be unfairly decided or taken away from you. Under ERISA, your plan must provide for survivors—such as spouses—by allowing you to choose to receive survivor benefits or to select high benefits for yourself that end at your death. The *Retirement Equity Act* requires that your spouse sign a written consent if he or she agrees to waive survivor benefits.

If you are denied benefits, your plan must give you the reason for denial in writing and in a manner you can understand. It also must give you a reasonable opportunity for a fair and full review of the decision by the plan trustees. You have at least sixty days (the plan may provide you with more time) in which to request a review (instructions for how to request it will be in the plan summary).

ERISA prohibits employers from firing employees to avoid paying a pension. If this happens to you, get an attorney and file a case in federal court.

If you have problems receiving payments from your plan, starting payments, or understanding your benefits, talk to your plan administrator. If you are unable to get problems resolved, contact the Department of Labor at **www.dol.gov** or 866-4-USA-DOL. You are entitled to seek legal representation to assist you with any problems you encounter.

BANK ACCOUNTS

While most people have checking or savings accounts, there are several other types of bank accounts you may wish to consider that can help make your life easier down the road.

Joint Checking Account

A joint checking account is an account that you share with another person, often a spouse or child. Either person may withdraw funds from or deposit funds into the account.

NOTE: *Both people on the account have the right to withdraw all the money in the account without consulting the other person.*

This kind of account is often the kind spouses share, but it can also be useful to share with an adult child so that he or she can simply write a check from that account should you need someone to pay bills for you. You may also wish to have a joint account if you are unmarried and living with someone. Paying household bills can be simplified if you have a joint account. This kind of account *can* affect Medicaid eligibility because it is an asset that is considered. If your spouse has a lot of money and your name is on the account, it is considered partially your money.

Pay on Death Account

Pay on death accounts, also known as *Totten Trusts*, are bank accounts that are owned by you during your lifetime but pass automatically to another person upon your death. During your lifetime, you can use the account as you would any other. However, upon your death, the account transfers without going through probate or any other proceeding. On the account papers, you should name the person you want the account transferred to. You can only name a qualifying person who must be related to you as a:

- spouse;
- child;
- grandchild;
- parent;
- brother;
- sister;
- half-sibling;
- stepbrother;
- stepsister; or,
- stepchild.

These accounts are insured up to $100,000. If you and a spouse jointly own a Totten Trust, it is considered as two accounts and is insured as such (for up to $200,000). If one spouse dies, the other has a six month grace period to change the person the account will go to upon the death of the surviving spouse while the full amount is insured.

PROPERTY TAX EXEMPTIONS

Property taxes can be the single greatest financial burden for seniors who own and live in their own homes. By this stage of a person's life, a homeowner is often mortgage free, but is usually living on a reduced income. Large yearly property tax bills can be very difficult to afford. Many states have recognized the burden this places on senior homeowners and created special reduced tax rates for seniors.

These tax relief programs have different names in different areas, but are often called *homestead exemptions*, *property tax credits*, or *property tax deferral programs*. To find out if your state or locality has such a program and to find out how to qualify and apply for it, contact your town hall, county office, or local property tax assessment office. Often, the paperwork is very simple and easy to complete. The tax breaks that are available can be very significant.

LIVING ON A FIXED INCOME

If you are retired, or plan to retire, and will rely on Social Security and/or a retirement account as your primary source of financial support, you will be living on a *fixed income*. A fixed income means that you will have a certain number of dollars available to you each month and nothing more—your income will not fluctuate. This means you will need to carefully budget your expenses, understand exactly how much money you have coming in each month, and be careful not to overspend.

SENIOR TIP

Read tips about living on a fixed income at:

http://ohioline.osu.edu/ss-fact/0159.html

To better manage this situation, create a budget. Make a complete list of all your monthly expenses, including utility bills, rent, food, insurance, taxes, medical costs (including prescriptions), transportation, entertainment, gifts, and so on. It is also a good idea to try to keep an *emergency fund*—money that you set aside for use when something unexpected comes up. Even if you have extensive savings available to you, you will want to try to protect those funds for future use and not spend them all early in your retirement years.

REVERSE MORTGAGES

A *reverse mortgage* is a financial arrangement in which you mortgage your home, but the bank or financial institution pays you a set amount of money every month while you continue to live in the home. You are in essence selling your equity to the bank in exchange for monthly payments or a large lump-sum payment. This can be a good solution for some seniors who cannot afford to keep their homes or live any other way. Be aware that by doing this, you will leave a home with a large mortgage on it. That is fine if you do not want to be able to pass your home on to your heirs.

This option can make more sense than a home equity loan in some cases because foreclosure is not an option and you do not have to try to make monthly payments to the bank. You can repay a reverse mortgage, but most people do not plan on doing so and see it as a way to sell their home, yet still have the comfort and convenience of living in it. A reverse mortgage also provides you with another way to obtain cash to pay for health care.

The *Federal Housing Authority* (FHA) insures some reverse mortgages under the *Home Equity Conversion Mortgage Demonstration* (HECMD). You must be 62 years old to qualify and own the home free and clear or have a low mortgage balance. There are no income requirements. These loans assume the home will appreciate 4% each year, but if it does not, the lender must continue to make payments until the full amount is paid. The department of *Housing and Urban Development* (HUD) insures the loan so if the lender cannot make payments, HUD will.

AFFORDING HEALTH CARE

Chapter 2 discusses health insurance, but many people find that their insurance plans do not provide coverage for all of their medical expenses. Seniors who do not qualify for Medicaid because they have too many assets may not have enough funds to pay for all the medical bills that they accrue.

There are options other than health insurance to pay for health care. You may be able to pay for care out of your savings. Most people do not have enough savings to do this and must consider other options. Some of these other options include using life insurance, annuities, and your home to increase the amount of funds available to you.

Living Benefits from Life Insurance

Some life insurance plans have *living benefits* (also called *accelerated benefits*) that allow the policy holder to begin collecting benefits to pay for long-term care or other health care. When you use accelerated benefits, you are getting an early payment of the death benefit your policy offers. When you die, they policy will not pay anything to your beneficiaries if you have used up your full accelerated benefit. Check with your insurer to see if this is available. *Riders* (or *amendments*) can be added to existing policies that do not contain this provision.

Viatical Settlements

Another method of using life insurance to get cash-in-hand now is *viatical settlements*. There are companies that will purchase your life insurance policy for a portion of the face value of it, and in return become the beneficiary of the policy, receiving the full death benefit at the time of death. However, this option is usually only available if you are terminally ill.

Viatical settlements require that:

- you are terminally ill;
- you allow the company to have access to your medical records to prove your life expectancy;
- you have owned the policy for at last two years; and,
- your beneficiary agrees to your plan to sell the policy.

This kind of arrangement allows you to get immediate cash, but when you sell your life insurance policy, it means that your beneficiaries will not receive payment from the policy when you die. Many families rely on life insurance policies to pay for funeral costs, but with viatical settlements those costs must be paid directly out of your estate, or by surviving family members.

To choose a reputable company for a viatical settlement:

- compare at least two offers—the more you can compare, the better deal you are sure to get;
- call your state attorney general's office to check for any complaints against the companies you are considering;
- request that the company place the purchase funds in escrow so that you know they exist and can be accessed by you once you sign over the policy;
- make sure payment will be made immediately upon signing the agreement; and,
- go over the settlement with your tax advisor and estate planning attorney before you agree to anything.

Annuities

You can sell your home and invest the proceeds in an *annuity* that will pay out a set amount each month. This is also known as a *Medicaid annuity* because you reduce the large value of your assets, qualifying you for Medicaid, but you still receive money every month for living expenses. This is different from a reverse mortgage because your entire home is being sold and you are left with ownership in an annuity. You must, of course, find other housing if you choose this option.

Some states have placed restrictions on these kinds of annuities. While annuities are usually poor investments, they do work to shelter assets from Medicaid. Carefully discuss this option with your estate planning attorney before making any decisions or commitments.

–2–

HEALTH INSURANCE

Most people agree that their health is their most precious commodity. Protecting your health and making sure you can access medical care is one of the most important things you can do to make your life satisfying and comfortable. It is no secret that health care in the United States is not always accessible or affordable for everyone. Recent publicity about Medicare reforms has made it clear that this is especially true for seniors. Finally, the right to quality, affordable medical care is becoming a major topic of consumer discussion.

This chapter addresses the health insurance options available to seniors. It also explains eligibility and how to use the kinds of insurance available to you.

TYPES OF INSURANCE

There are different types of health insurance. While each type has different requirements and is run by different entities, it is important to realize that many people combine one or more types of coverage to meet their needs. It can be confusing to deal with different types of coverage, but you usually have more protection this way. The three general types of health insurance coverage discussed in the following sections are Medicare, Medicaid, and private health insurance policies.

Medicare is a federally funded health insurance program designed to help pay seniors' health-care costs. It has two parts, *Part A*, which covers hospitalization, and *Part B*, which covers doctor visits.

Medicaid is a health insurance program run by the individual states for low-income individuals (seniors included) and is supposed to be an insurance of *last resort*. You may have heard of having to *spend down to Medicaid*. This means a person must use up most of his or her assets in order to qualify.

Private health insurance policies are the kind provided by employers or purchased by an individual. These policies are provided by private health insurance companies and the premiums are paid for by employers or by the *insured* (the people covered by the policies). Some of these privately purchased policies are called *Medigap*, which means they are designed to specifically cover things Medicare does not. *Long-term care insurance* is private insurance purchased specifically to cover the cost of *assisted living* and *nursing home care*. (These options are discussed in Chapter 5.)

MEDICARE

Medicare is a federal benefit that accrues according to earnings the same way Social Security benefits accrue. For every year you work, your eligibility increases. A person is eligible for Medicare at age 65 and can apply three months prior to his or her 65th birthday. People already receiving Social Security benefits are automatically enrolled one month before their 65th birthday. You are also eligible if you are under 65 and have been permanently and totally disabled for at least 24 months.

If you are not eligible through your earnings history, you can purchase Medicare as long as you are within the age requirements. You cannot be denied coverage because of your medical history.

To enroll for Medicare (or for Social Security), call 800-772-1213 or visit your local Social Security office (check the government pages of your phone book for locations). Even if you have no immediate plans to use Medicare coverage, it is a good idea to enroll and become part of the system as soon as you are eligible so that you have the paperwork out of the way and can access benefits immediately should you need them.

Administration

The federal government contracts Medicare to private health insurance programs that then administer the benefits. Your Medicare plan may be handled by Blue Cross, for example, or some other local health insurance company. *Health Maintenance Organizations* (HMOs) also handle Medicare. If you are covered by an HMO for Medicare, you will need to select a *primary care doctor* and follow the HMO's rules for referrals to specialists. Having your Medicare plan administered by an HMO offers benefits, such as better access to care, but also has the detriment of creating another layer of administration to deal with. A *Medicare cost plan* allows you to choose where you will receive care, but you will have to pay more out of pocket. You may also choose a *preferred provider organization* (PPO). This plan allows you to use your primary care provider as a gateway for all care.

Coverage

Medicare has strict regulations about what *types of care* it covers and how much it pays. Medicare decides how much your doctor is paid for the treatment you receive—not the doctor. The doctor cannot charge you more than Medicare will pay, if you are covered by Medicare and the doctor accepts Medicare. Because of this possible fee limitation, many doctors will not accept Medicare patients. It can be particularly difficult to find care providers for seniors in rural areas or who are without transportation.

To find doctors who participate in Medicare, use the online search tool at **www.medicare.gov/Physician/Home.asp** or contact your local Medicare office for assistance. (See Appendix B for more information.)

There are many things Medicare does not cover, such as:

- extended nursing home stays (stays of up to 90 days are covered in part);
- glasses;
- hearing aids;
- check-ups (currently only one physical is covered when you enroll in the program);
- private nursing care; and,
- dental care.

Be aware that the list of covered items changes yearly and often expands. Check with your local Medicare office or with your doctor to find out if a treatment that is proposed or necessary will be covered. There is a co-pay for almost everything covered under Medicare.

Part A and Part B

Medicare coverage is broken into two types or parts. *Part A* covers hospital stays (and limited nursing home stays) and is a benefit that is offered free of charge. *Part B* covers doctor visits, tests, medical equipment, and some prescriptions.

A monthly *premium* (payment) must be paid to receive Part B benefits. In 2004 it was $66.60, but this may be higher depending on when you signed up. The new rates are sent to you each January. The premium can be directly deducted from Social Security benefits or paid out-of-pocket. There is also an annual deductible and a co-payment for most services.

Subscribing to Part B is optional and a person can choose not to accept the coverage at the time he or she signs up for Part A. However, the premium can go up 10% each year, and if a person chooses to sign up for Part B later, he or she will have to pay the premium increases. Additionally, there is a limited window of opportunity open each year to sign up for Part B coverage. Open enrollment is only available from January 1 through April 1 or the three months before you turn 65. If you are already receiving Social Security benefits, you are automatically enrolled in Part B when you turn 65.

Deciding whether or not to purchase Part B benefits is an individual choice. It must be made by looking at what other types of insurance you have or are eligible for, as well as thinking about your health and financial situation.

SENIOR TIP

Qualified Medicare Beneficiary Program pays Medicare premiums and co-pays for seniors who have low incomes and few assets. For more information, Read *Medicare Saving Programs*, available at your local Social Security office or online at: **www.medicare.gov/Publications**

In the future, you may have the option of establishing a *Medical Savings Account*, but unfortunately to date, this option has not been made available. Medicare laws established that this would be available to 390,000 Medicare beneficiaries. The beneficiaries would be able to purchase Medical Savings Accounts as part of a test program. The beneficiary would choose a *Medicare Medical Savings Account (MSA)* (a health insurance policy with a high deductible). Medicare would pay the premium for the MSA and make a deposit into the Medicare MSA that is established by the beneficiary. The beneficiary would use the funds in the Medicare MSA to pay for services provided before the deductible is met and for other services not covered by the MSA. This option has not yet been put into effect, but it is something to be aware of.

SENIOR TIP

If you need to replace your Medicare card, call 800-772-1213.

Prescriptions

Coverage for prescriptions under Medicare begins in 2006. It will be optional at a cost of $35 a year. Under the plan, there will be a $250 yearly deductible and coverage for 75% of costs up to $2250. Coverage will not be available for costs between $2252 and $5100. Ninety-five percent of costs over $5100 will be covered. Low-income seniors will have additional coverage and lower out-of-pocket costs. Until the coverage takes effect, Medicare participants have the option of purchasing a *prescription drug discount card* to help reduce prescription costs.

SENIOR TIP

An online calculator that can help you understand how the Medicare legislation will impact your prescription costs can be found at:

http://sites.stockpoint.com/AARP/drugbenefit.asp

Appeals

Although there are certain types of care Medicare does not cover, you always have the right to appeal a decision by Medicare not to pay your claim. The claim must be *submitted* (this is done through the participating doctor) and *denied* before you can appeal.

Even though many things are obviously not covered, you must first wait for the claim to be submitted and denied before you can begin your appeal. The denial forms include instructions for how to appeal the decision. Your doctor also handles the appeal.

SENIOR TIP

Find a listing of state-by-state pharmacy assistance programs at:

www.aarp.org/bulletin/yourmoney/Articles/

Once an appeal is begun, Part B claims are then subject to *review*. A review is the process Medicare goes through to determine if something should have been paid for under its coverage. Appeals must be submitted within six months of the denial and are decided within eight weeks of submission. If the review denies coverage, then you are entitled to a *fair hearing*.

A fair hearing is an informal administrative hearing where you can present your position and argue for why the claim should be covered. You have six months to request a fair hearing after a denial resulting from the review. This is held at an office—not in front of a judge. The hearing is recorded and transcribed.

Part A claims for in-patient hospital care that have been denied are heard by a *peer review organization* (a group of doctors who determine if the claim should be covered). You have sixty days from denial to request this review and a decision is made within thirty days (ten days for nursing home care).

Both Part A and Part B denials that are not resolved by the mentioned appeal processes can proceed to an administrative hearing before an *administrative law judge* (called an ALJ). You have sixty days from denial of the appeal to request this hearing. Your claim must be for a minimum of $500 for Part B benefits or $200 for Part A benefits to have a hearing before an ALJ. If the ALJ denies the claim, it goes to the Social Security Appeals Council Review, where sworn testimony and evidence is

SENIOR TIP

Your local Social Security office can help you appeal a Medicare decision. You can locate an attorney experienced in handling these matters through The National Organization of Social Security Claimants' Representatives (NOSSCR) at 800-431-2804 or **www.nosscr.org**. (It is a very good idea to use an attorney to help you navigate the appeals process.)

taken in a formal proceeding. If this is denied, it can be appealed to federal court.

If you are in a hospital and Medicare denies a claim that would allow you to stay in the hospital, you must request a review of the decision by noon on the day of your planned discharge. The claim is then heard by a peer review organization.

You have an absolute right to appeal a decision that denies coverage, but more than likely you will only be given coverage for items that are clearly within Medicare's payment guidelines. While your care might have been important, necessary, or unavoidable, Medicare will not pay for anything not specifically covered.

Tips for Handling a Medicaid or Medicare Hearing or Appeal

- Dress formally.
- Bring an attorney if you can afford one.
- Bring a family member or friend for support.
- Bring all of your medical records with you.
- Have your medical records organized in an accessible way.
- Bring a letter from your doctor explaining the medical condition and the needed treatment.
- Speak calmly and politely.
- Be patient and wait your turn.
- Obtain copies of all documents that are issued at or after the hearing.
- Do not be afraid to ask to have things explained or repeated to you.

MEDICAID

Medicaid is an insurance program designed to provide health insurance to individuals, including seniors, with low incomes. Most people who receive *Supplemental Security Income* (SSI) are also eligible for and automatically receive Medicaid. Medicaid receives funding from the states and the federal government, but is administered by each state individually. This means that each state has its own plans, rules, and regulations.

Eligibility

Medicaid *eligibility* is determined by looking at a person's income and assets. When considering eligibility, certain personal assets are considered *exempt* and are therefor not included in the calculation of a person's income. Such exempt assets include a person's:

- home;
- wedding rings;
- burial plot;
- car;
- personal and household belongings (up to about $2000); and,
- life insurance policies with a total cash value under $5000.

Everything is evaluated by your state's standards to determine eligibility. To qualify, generally you must receive only a few hundred dollars of income per month and have a small amount of savings—no more than a few thousand dollars. You need to check your own state's rules for eligibility, because the rules do vary. For assistance, contact your local Medicaid office or your local agency on aging.

Medicaid coverage is important because it is often the only way that people of middle or low incomes can afford *long-term care*, such as nursing home care. Because this care is so expensive, most people are not able to pay for years of care on their own, and at some point must rely on Medicaid to cover the bills.

In some states there is no income limit for Medicaid eligibility. However, those states usually require that any of the senior's income over a certain amount be paid directly to the nursing home, with Medicaid then paying whatever balance remains on the monthly care bill.

Medicaid recipients can keep some income for their personal use and to care for their homes. Medicaid calculates income according to the name on the check. If a check is payable to you, it is your income. If it is payable to your spouse, it is not your income as far as Medicaid is concerned.

To apply for Medicaid, you must provide financial records and proof of assets and expenses. Financial records for the previous thirty-six months before applying (known as the *look-back period*) are considered during the application process. This is important to remember, because many people incorrectly think they can *transfer* assets to relatives in order to qualify.

NOTE: *The transfer rules are very complicated, and if you are considering trying to arrange your assets in order to qualify, it is important that you talk to a financial planner who is experienced in this area.*

Applications

Many people become eligible for Medicaid by *spending down* to it. In other words, many people use up their own assets to pay health care bills until they have so little left that they qualify for Medicaid. Becoming eligible for Medicaid is quite tricky and cannot be done simply by giving things away to family members. Medicaid planning is a big business. Talk to an attorney who handles Medicaid planning. There are certain devices you can use to help you qualify, such as trusts, so do not simply assume that you do not qualify. Get the facts from your attorney and discuss what you can do in order to qualify.

Application decisions are made within forty-five days of the application date. To apply for Medicaid, speak to the *patient advocate* or social worker at the hospital or facility where you are staying or contact your local agency on aging. (see Appendix D .) Use a professional Medicaid planner to help you apply if there are any questions at all about your assets or transfers you have made. Make sure you write down the name and phone number of the Medicaid agency application counselor you meet with. It may take several visits or phone calls for you to provide him or her with all of the necessary information.

Medicaid Transfers

Because Medicaid is designed to provide coverage for people with low incomes, there are rules in place to make sure people do not just give away their assets to become eligible. If these rules did not exist, even a millionaire could transfer all of his or her assets to a relative today and become eligible for Medicaid tomorrow. That is why Medicaid examines the past thirty-six months.

Be aware that transferring assets that are not exempt will create a *period of ineligibility*. To calculate the length of this period, you must take the amount of the transfer and divide it by the average monthly cost of nursing home care in your area. The result is the number of months you are ineligible from the date of the transfer.

> ***Example:*** If you transfer a mutual fund worth $20,000 to your son in January and then apply for Medicaid, the $20,000 is divided by the average nursing home cost per month in your area (use $2000 for this example). Dividing the $20,000 by the $2,000 monthly cost for nursing home care results in you being ineligible for Medicaid for ten months. Therefore, you would be ineligible for coverage until November of that year, even though you do not own the mutual fund anymore and may have no way to pay your nursing home bills.

You can see why it is important to use a Medicaid planner to help you understand your eligibility.

Medicaid recipients can pay family members for services they perform for them as long as the payment is reasonable. For example, it would be reasonable to pay your daughter $25 a week to do your laundry, but $200 a week would not be reasonable.

You have the right to transfer the assets that are exempt whenever you want without affecting your eligibility. There are, however, rules restricting when homes and nonexempt assets may be transferred. An unmarried person can transfer his or her home to a minor or disabled child. He or she could also transfer the home to a child if the purpose of the transfer was other than to qualify for Medicaid. The home can also be transferred to a child who lived in it the previous two years to care for the parent, or if the child has an ownership interest in the home and lived there one year prior.

A married person can transfer the home to his or her spouse (who can then transfer it to the children without affecting eligibility). A married person can also transfer any nonexempt asset to his or her spouse, but the spouse receiving it cannot transfer it within thirty-six months for less than its full value.

Transfers can be planned to maximize eligibility yet minimize the amount a person must spend in order to become eligible.

Some options include:

- investing money in the home (such as paying off the mortgage or improving it);
- taking a *life estate* in the home and giving a *remainder interest* to your child (which means you have control over it as long as you live, but your child automatically owns it when you die);
- transferring assets between spouses while there are still two spouses alive; and,
- placing assets in an *irrevocable trust* to protect them.

It is important to consult an attorney who specializes in this area to be sure you are making the best choices and following the law.

Some people get divorced to protect assets from Medicaid. The spouse who does not need Medicaid coverage takes all of the nonexempt assets, protecting them from Medicaid consideration. They are then not counted as belonging to the spouse using

Medicaid. Being divorced does not mean you cannot live together, so some couples divorce only in name to protect their assets from Medicaid. This may seem like a drastic solution, but it makes financial sense to some people.

NOTE: *If you divorce you may not be able to collect Social Security survivor benefits on behalf of your spouse, so this is a decision that you must weigh carefully.*

State Medicaid programs have systems in place called *estate recovery plans*. These plans operate by the state placing a *lien* (a legal hold against the property) in the amount of the person's medical costs against the home, even though a person may be permitted to keep his or her home and still be eligible for Medicaid. The state will then require a sale or a cash payment to satisfy the lien after the person dies. The state cannot force a sale of the home while a spouse or minor or disabled child still lives there. The state can also seek reimbursement from the deceased's estate for the amount owed.

Spouses

The spouse of a person receiving Medicaid is permitted to keep some assets without applying them towards the other spouse's medical care. He or she may keep:

- all income in his or her name;
- $2100 a month of income in the other spouse's name, if more than half of the couple's income is in the other spouse's name;
- the home;
- the *community spouse resource amount* (one half of all liquid assets, up to $84,000 in some states);
- a car;
- the furniture and household goods;

- the wedding rings;
- a life insurance policy with a face value of up to $1500; and,
- two burial plots with savings account for burial up to $1500.

Coverage

Medicaid coverage is broader than Medicare. However, obtaining care can sometimes be more difficult. Medicaid covers prescriptions, nursing home care, home health care, doctor visits, and hospitalization. Some state plans also cover dental care, eye care, hospice care, and therapy. Contact your local agency on aging for information about your state plan.

The problem with Medicaid is that it can be difficult to find a provider. All hospitals are required to accept Medicaid, but nursing homes that choose to accept Medicaid have a certain number of available beds for Medicaid patients. Many doctors will not accept Medicaid patients, forcing Medicaid patients to use busy clinics with long waiting times.

Medicaid provides *retroactive coverage* for nursing home care for up to three months before you apply for Medicaid, as long as you would have been eligible during that time period. The facility providing coverage must accept Medicaid payment as payment-in-full.

SENIOR TIP

For more details about Medicaid coverage, go to:

www.thebeehive.org/health/contests/medicaid.asp

or

www.cms.hhs.gov/medicaid/consumer.asp?

Not all facilities have to accept Medicaid. Only *certified providers* must accept Medicaid payment. Medicaid provides unlimited coverage for nursing home stays and for assisted living (if assisted living is covered by the state Medicaid program).

Appeals

To appeal a denial of Medicaid coverage, you must receive a *notice of a reduction in benefits*. You have ten days to respond to it and request a hearing. You are entitled to a fair hearing in front of a *hearing officer* within ninety days of your request. Your benefits must be continued during this time. The hearing is an informal administrative proceeding. The government must show that it followed the law in denying coverage. You have the right to appear, have an attorney, and call witnesses. A detailed letter about your condition and treatment from your doctor is an important piece of evidence to bring to a hearing. If you are denied coverage in the fair hearing, you need to follow your state's individual procedures for appeals. These vary from state to state. Contact your local agency on aging for details on your state's procedures.

PRIVATE INSURANCE

Many people choose traditional private insurance as a way to protect their assets, since Medicaid coverage is not available until assets are spent down to a certain amount. *Medigap* is also appealing because there are so many things not covered by Medicare. Medigap policies may pay Medicare premiums, co-pays, and deductibles. It is best to purchase a Medigap policy no later than six months after enrolling in Medicare. After this time period, insurers can deny coverage based on pre-existing conditions. Additionally, many people carry private insurance policies as part of retirement plans, which are not purchased specifically as Medigap plans.

SENIOR TIP

For more information on the ten standard plans, visit:

www.doi.state.id.us/shiba/medigap.aspx

Types of Medigap Plans

There are ten standard Medigap plans. All ten plans are not offered in all states. Each plan offers varying levels of coverage. All must include at a minimum:

- 60–90 days of hospital coverage with a lifetime reserve of 91–150 days;
- 365 days of hospital coverage after Medicare reimbursements;
- Part B physician coinsurance; and,
- three pints of blood per year.

Plans *may* include coverage for:

- skilled nursing care;
- Part A and Part B deductibles;
- parts of bills not covered by Medicare;
- drugs; and,
- preventive care.

The premiums vary. It is important to note that once the Medicare prescription coverage becomes available (see p.20), existing Medigap policies that cover prescriptions will continue to do so, but new policies will no longer include this coverage. There are no plans to allow Medigap policies to cover prescription drug costs not covered by the new Medicare plan.

To purchase a Medigap policy, check with your insurance agent or with well-known local health insurance companies. You can obtain a list of companies from your state agency on aging.

When seeking Medigap coverage, ask which plan you are being offered and get complete details about the type of coverage that will be provided. Complete all applications carefully and include all information requested. Read the policy carefully and understand what it covers exactly. Look for:

- the levels of care covered;
- the length of the waiting period before the policy begins to pay;
- any requirement that Medicare approve the care before this policy pays (you will not want a policy with such a requirement);
- any benefit limits;
- a provision that the policy is guaranteed to be renewable;
- a provision offering inflation protection;
- set premiums;
- a provision waiving premiums once you begin to use the policy;
- no requirement for a hospital stay before benefits to kick in; and,
- policy delivery within thirty days of purchase.

SENIOR TIP

The Medicare site has a free personal Medicare health-care plan finder that helps you compare Medigap policies and evaluate your Medicare coverage. Go to:

www.medicare.gov/MPPF/Home.asp

You have thirty days to review a policy, choose not to accept it, and get a full refund.

There are private insurance policies that are not Medigap policies, so be clear on what you are buying. Always ask which of the ten types you are buying so you are clear that it is a Medigap policy. You can also evaluate private insurance companies by looking them up in *A.M. Best,* an insurance rating book that can be found at your local library.

SENIOR TIP

Read more about Medigap coverage at:

www.aarp.org/healthcoverage/medigap

LONG-TERM CARE INSURANCE

Because nursing home care can cost over $70,000 per year, long-term care insurance is an important tool for those who do not qualify for Medicaid and do not wish to have to *spend down* to become eligible. If a person is close to being eligible for Medicaid, it does not make much sense to purchase a long-term care policy.

As a general rule, the younger a person is when he or she purchases long-term care insurance, the more sense it makes. It may make more sense for you to invest the amount of the premiums and then use these funds to pay your health-care expenses. A rule of thumb that is often used is that if the premiums are 5% or less of your income, then the policy is a good investment. Be aware that premiums rise over time, so you must be sure that it will never be more than 5% of your income.

Studies have shown that if a prior hospitalization is required to activate the policy (which is often the case), there is more than a 50% chance you will never be able to collect any money from the policy. If only skilled care is reimbursed, there is a 45% chance that you will never need to collect.

Plans are usually not available to those over age 80 and may be quite expensive for those in their 70s. It may make more sense to save the amount premiums would cost and use them to save for in-home care.

Long-term care policies only remain in effect as long as premiums are paid. However, most policies contain a *waiver for premiums due* while the insured is receiving long-term care. This means you do not pay while receiving benefits.

Evaluate a long-term care policy by checking to see exactly what kind of care it covers. Examine it by asking the following questions.

- Does it cover in-home care by nurses and personal care aides?
- Does it cover skilled and unskilled nursing home care?

- Are there restrictions and prerequisites for coverage, such as requiring a hospital stay prior to covering nursing home care?
- Is there a *waiting period* (sometimes called an *elimination* or *reduction period*) before benefits will be paid?
- Is there inflation protection (with the policy limits increasing with inflation)?
- Is there a return of premium if you die prior to a set age (70 is often used)?
- Is there an exclusion for Alzheimer's or other brain disorders and impairment?
- What reimbursement levels and maximum benefits are allowed in the policy and are they enough to cover all nursing home or in-home care?
- What are the maximum pay-outs? (Most policies have a limit on how much care they will cover, such as 100 days of nursing home care at a time or two years total skilled nursing care. The higher the limit, the more expensive the premiums will be.)
- Are the premiums fixed and set at a single amount per month or do they vary?
- What is the cancellation policy? (Make sure the policy can only be cancelled for nonpayment and for no other reason.)
- Is there *nonforfeiture protection* (a provision that allows some kind of refund of a percent of premiums paid should you cancel the policy)?
- Is policy guaranteed as renewable so that it cannot be cancelled?

Check on the financial stability of the company. (Use *A.M. Best* to do this—it is a book your local library will have.) If the company goes bankrupt, the premiums you have paid will be for nothing.

SENIOR TIP

A shopper's guide to long-term care insurance is available from:

NAIC Insurance Products and Services Division
2301 McGee Street, Suite 800
Kansas City, MO 64108
Phone: 816-783-8300
http://www.naic.org/insprod/catalog_pub_consumer.htm

SENIOR TIP

Activities of Daily Living include:

- bathing;
- eating;
- dressing;
- changing positions; and,
- toileting.

Find out if your state has a state-certified long-term care insurance program. These special state-sponsored programs allow you to purchase long-term care insurance and qualify for Medicaid with a larger amount of assets than is normally permitted. Contact your local agency on aging for information on this. (see Appendix D.)

Eligibility

Long-term care policies usually kick into effect when you need assistance with two or more activities of daily living (ADL). A policy that requires more than three ADLs should be avoided since you will probably need care before the policy kicks in.

–3–

HEALTH CARE

Because everyone wants to remain healthy and active, medical care and medical assistance are vital parts of our lives. Understanding your health care rights will help you make the most of the care you receive and do so in an informed and knowledgeable way.

CHOOSING HEALTH-CARE PROVIDERS

Your primary health-care provider is the person who links you to most medical care, monitors any conditions you have, and helps you look toward the future care you might need. Finding a provider you trust, can talk to, and one who will be open and honest with you is one of the most important steps you can take to protect your health.

Unfortunately, there may be limits on who you can select as your primary health-care provider. Private health insurance often restricts care to providers who participate in their program. Medicare is often administered through private home maintenance organizations (HMOs) that restrict who a senior can see for health care. Medicaid recipients must see Medicaid providers.

If you are beginning your coverage under a new insurance program, choose a provider from the list of providers available to you through your health insurance plan. Obtain a provider directory from your insurance company. If you currently have a provider that you would like to continue to see, call the provider and ask if he or she participates in your new plan.

Many HMO's and private insurance plans make a distinction between primary care providers and specialists. An internist would be considered a primary care provider, but a rheumatologist or urologist would be a specialist.

Many plans require *referrals* from the primary care provider to a specialist if the specialist's care is to be covered. If you have specialists that you presently see, it makes sense to ask a new primary care provider to process referrals to them so that you can have *continuity of care* with your specialists.

When choosing providers, ask yourself the following questions.

- Is this provider polite and easy to understand?
- Are waiting times to see this provider acceptable?
- Is the provider accessible to me with the transportation I have available?
- Does he or she listen to my questions and answer them?
- Am I given enough time with the provider?
- Is the provider's staff friendly and polite?
- Is the provider's office handicap accessible?
- Does the provider accept my insurance?

If you wish to see a provider who is not covered by your insurance plan, you still may be able to do so. Ask about *out-of-network* or nonparticipating provider plans. You may be required to pay a percentage of the bill, with your insurance plan picking up the rest.

You will want to know about the rules regarding out-of-network care as well for when you travel. Should you become ill and need to see a doctor or go to a hospital, your plan probably offers coverage of some kind.

INFORMED CONSENT

Informed consent is a guideline that providers must follow. It requires them to fully inform patients about the risks, benefits, side effects, and possible outcomes of any medical treatment. While this sounds like a simple proposition, it is actually very complicated. For example, how many times have you gone for an x-ray or received a flu shot without anyone giving you a detailed explanation of what will happen; how it could affect you; and, what the possible outcomes could be? It is not likely that anyone discussed the dangers of radiation with you before an x-ray or warned you that you might have a severe reaction to the flu shot. There are risks associated with almost every kind of medical care, from minor office care to major hospital care. Simply put, it is too difficult for care providers to warn you of all the possible dangers for every single treatment.

What you should expect is that your provider will fully explain any procedure, treatment, or medication to you and will detail any important risks it poses. As a patient, your role should be to ask any questions about it that come to your mind. Get your provider to tell you all the risks, all the possible outcomes, and all the alternative treatments by asking for this information. Informed consent requires your provider to be up front with you, but does not require him or her to give you extremely detailed information. Always ask if you want to know more.

SECOND OPINIONS

A *second opinion* is a good way to verify information or suggestions that you are being given about your medical care. When you are facing surgery or have been given a serious diagnosis, a second opinion can provide a check on the information you are given, as well as offer a different point of view and additional information.

Most insurance plans allow you to obtain a second opinion from a participating physician. Keep in mind that you may need to see several physicians in different specialties in some situations to get a complete picture of your condition. This is covered as well, since each specialist will be dealing with a different effect or symptom of the same problem.

Many insurers actually require a second opinion before some surgeries or expensive treatments. Getting a second opinion is your right. It is usually important that you bring test results, x-rays, and medical records with you so that the second physician has something to work with. If you believe some test results are erroneous, ask to have them repeated.

MEDICAL PRIVACY

The *Health Insurance Portability and Accountability Act* (HIPAA) is a federal law that lays out a patient's right to privacy with regard to his or her medical records. The law states that health-care providers must have a system in place to provide security for medical records.

Health-care information cannot be disclosed to your employer or to anyone else (except another health-care provider that is caring for you). This means that you must complete a *release* to grant a spouse, child, or other relative access to your health-care information or records. Psychotherapy notes are included in this and have the additional protection of not being able to be released to an insurance company without the patient's permission. The insurance company cannot deny benefits if notes are not provided.

When you are hospitalized, you have the right to have your name removed from the hospital directory and can choose not to allow the hospital to release any information about your status.

Every health-care provider or organization must have a designated *privacy officer*—a person who is in charge of privacy protections. If you believe your privacy rights have been violated, you need to contact this person with your concerns. If your complaint is unresolved or not resolved to your satisfaction, contact:

U.S. Department of Health and Human Services
Office for Civil Rights
200 Independence Avenue, S.W.
Washington, DC 20201
202-619-0257
or 877-696-6775
www.hhs.gov/ocr/hipaa

Make sure you file your complaint within 180 days of the incident. The Department of Health and Human Services can impose civil and criminal penalties upon the health-care provider. You personally do not have the right to sue a provider for a violation of this law.

SENIOR TIP

For more information about health privacy or to obtain information about filing a complaint, visit **www.healthprivacy.org**.

You may also want to contact your state attorney general (**www.naag.org**), state insurance commissioner (**www.naic.org**), or your state medical board (**www.fsmb.org**).

Appointments

Many seniors like to have a family member or close friend come with them on medical appointments. It is absolutely your right to bring another person with you on an appointment or consultation. Additionally, many seniors find that it is helpful for them to have a family member or friend who can call doctors if there are problems or request additional information. Especially when you are ill, it is nice to know there is someone who can ask questions, get test results, and manage things for you. However, in order for this to happen, you must sign a consent form. Your care provider may have a preferred form or you can use the one provided in Appendix G.

MEDICAL RECORDS

You have the right to see and add to your own medical records. You also have the right to obtain copies of your medical records within thirty days of your request. However, most physicians charge a fee for copying. The *American Medical Association* (AMA) suggests that physicians charge a *reasonable fee*. Many states have laws governing this, but others simply say the fee must be reasonable. Some states do provide specific per-page fees or limit the retrieval fees.

SENIOR TIP

To see the list of approved state fees for copying medical records, visit: **http://library.ahima.org/xpedio/groups/public/documents/ahima/pub_bok1_000052.html.**

It is important that you obtain copies of all:

- test results;
- diagnoses;
- treatment plans; and,
- blood work.

If you decide to seek a second opinion, you will have a complete file to take with you.

AGAINST MEDICAL ADVICE

As a patient, you have the right to make medical decisions for yourself and to refuse treatment, even if it means you will die. If they believe it is a life-saving treatment, most physicians will try to convince you to follow their recommendation. But the final decision rests with you.

When in the hospital, you have the right to leave at any time. This is often referred to as signing out *against medical advice* (AMA). While you have the absolute right to make your own decisions about this, it is important to understand that if you do sign out AMA, your insurance company may refuse to pay for later treatment that results from this decision. So if you choose to leave immediately after surgery and then you develop an infection and must be

SENIOR TIP

Should you travel, you will have all information with you if you need to seek treatment. It is also important to keep an up-to-date list of prescriptions, with the name of the drug, reason for taking it, and dosage.

readmitted, your insurance can deny coverage for the second admission if it is caused by your actions.

Because of this, the best course of action is usually to have a conversation with your medical-care provider about why you want to leave. Listen to his or her reasons for wanting to keep you there and see if you can reach some kind of compromise (such as, *I will go home, but my daughter will move in with me for a week*). Many physicians are willing to be flexible and listen to a patient's feelings and needs.

HEALTH-CARE DIRECTIVES

A *health-care directive* is a legal document that specifies what medical treatment you will accept should you become unable to communicate or make your own decisions. These documents also name a person that you choose to make decisions for you, should you be unable to make them yourself.

Many people think they do not need a health-care directive because they believe that their health-care providers will do what is best for them; are in denial that something could happen to them; or, think that they would want to live and accept any treatment no matter what. In fact, if they think carefully about the realities of the situation, that may not be the case. Unfortunately, the risk of becoming unable to make your own medical decisions is real, and no one knows who will need a health-care directive. While health-care providers are supposed to do what is best for the patient, they cannot withhold treatment without a legal document permitting them to do so, even if it is what the patient would have wanted. People who think they do not need a health-care directive because they would want any treatment available often do not consider the many scenarios that are possible in which a body can live for years without any brain activity, putting a drain on the family's financial and emotional resources.

There are many different names for health-care directives, often called *living wills*. These documents can be long and comprehensive, describing in detail the type of care the patient will not consent to, or a simple one-page document. Living wills often discuss treatments such as feeding tubes, respirators, resuscitation, and pain medication. The details depend on your own personal wishes and how specific you wish to be. A *health-care proxy* is a document appointing a person who will make decisions for you if you are unable to make decisions for yourself. An *advance directive* usually contains the provisions of both living wills and health-care proxies.

Each state has its own laws about what forms and documents need to be completed, so it is important that you complete a form that is accepted in your state. An attorney can draft a document that directly addresses your wishes and can pose questions and scenarios to you that you might not have thought through on your own. (See Chapter 8 for more detailed information.)

SENIOR TIP

State-specific advance directives can be obtained through The Partnership for Caring at 800-989-9455 or **www.partnershipforcaring.org**.

If you have a living will, you may wish to file it with the US Living Will Registry:

www.livingwillregistry.com

HOSPITAL VISITATION ACCESS

Should you ever need to enter the hospital and you have nonfamily members that you would like to be able to visit you, it is important to mention this to your physician and to the admitting clerk. If you are unconscious, your relatives will be the ones who have the power to decide who will be permitted to see you. If you have someone special in your life, but you are not married (as is the case with many seniors), you may wish to consider writing a short statement indicating that you give that person permission to visit you and have access to you. File it with the hospital when you check in or give it to that person to use should he or she ever need it.

AFFORDING PRESCRIPTIONS

Amendments about prescription coverage to the Medicare law were made recently because prescriptions are so expensive and so essential for many seniors. But, as you learned when reading about this in Chapter 2, Medicare does not provide complete coverage for prescriptions and still requires a lot of out-of-pocket payments by seniors. Seniors who are covered by private insurance plans may have prescription coverage that makes the medications more affordable, and those on Medicaid are covered by their state plans.

Many seniors are looking for ways to reduce the cost of their prescriptions. Purchasing drugs in Canada is one option many seniors (and now many states and municipalities) consider. Canada has government-imposed price restrictions on pharmaceuticals, making their prices lower than ours. However, under current laws, it is not legal to import (or technically reimport, since most of these drugs were manufactured in the U.S.) drugs yourself—only manufacturers are permitted to do so.

Until recently, authorities have chosen to ignore importation of prescriptions by private citizens. The *Food and Drug Administration* (FDA) has begun to stop some large reimportation, citing safety concerns. Drugs that do not carry U.S. labels or that are not approved by name in the U.S. may be stopped. Currently, a bill is pending in Congress that would permit reimportation of drugs into the U.S. It is important that you understand the concerns the FDA

SENIOR TIP

If you are interested in buying drugs in Canada, look for pharmacies that are accredited by the *North American PCA*, which checks everything from how staff is hired to how the drugs are sent out. Contact them at:

North American PCA
PO Box 1146
Manchester, VT 05254
800-677-7019
http://na-pca.org/Impact

> **SENIOR TIP**
>
> If you need regular prescriptions but have limited transportation, consider using a local pharmacy that will deliver or order from an online drugstore that will mail your regular prescriptions and medical supplies to your home. You need a prescription for online drug orders. Sites that offer online diagnosis and prescriptions are not going to be able to provide adequate medical care.

has and make an informed decision. If you purchase drugs in Canada, you still need a prescription from your health-care provider.

MEDICAL TRIALS

If you are suffering from an illness or condition for which there is no complete cure or treatment, you probably feel frustrated by the lack of progress that is being made in researching and treating your condition.

Although there may not be an approved, widely-available treatment, there may be an experimental treatment that is currently being tested. Clinical trials of medication are done once a medication has been approved for trials on humans by the FDA. Participating in a trial not only helps to advance the research for your condition, but also possibly gives you the opportunity to take a medication that can help you. What you must understand about clinical trials is that most of them are done as double blinds, meaning neither the patient nor the treating physician knows who gets the medication being tested and who gets a placebo medication that has no medical effect and is used as a control factor. For many, though, this is a risk worth taking.

There is currently no complete database or listing of experimental trials for things other than prescriptions. However, there are many experimental therapies, treatments, and procedures that are being explored for many different conditions. If you are interested in finding out about cutting-edge or experimental treatments, first talk to your physician. Then contact the organization or foundation for your disease or condition (such as the *American Lung Association* for emphysema or the *National Digestive Diseases Foundation* for colitis) and ask them for information about alternative or experimental treatments. Some seniors explore options such as chiropractors and alternative medicine when nothing else works.

SENIOR TIP

A list of all clinical trials currently available in the U.S. and more information for how to apply to participate is available at **www.ClinicalTrials.gov**.

While there is no central database for nonprescription trials, for things like new or experimental procedures or therapies you can obtain information about them from:

National Institutes of Health
National Center for Complementary and Alternative Medicine Clearinghouse
P. O. Box 8218
Silver Spring, MD 20907-8218
1-888-644-6226
http://nccam.nih.gov

STAYING HEALTHY AT HOME

Remaining at home is perhaps the greatest goal shared by seniors as they age and face medical conditions. It is your right to live at home as long as you wish, but it is important to make sure you will be safe and well cared for before making this decision. Home modifications can help make your home safe and comfortable for you as long as you wish to live there. Modifications can include handrails, larger knobs on stoves, larger telephone buttons, nightlights, medical alert systems, removal of area rugs, and more. Medicare and Medicaid provide some funding for home modifications if they are medically necessary. The Department of Energy provides some funding to help weatherize homes. Weatherizing can include insulating and weather-proofing windows, as well as improving air flow. For more information about home modifications, contact your local agency on aging (see Appendix D.)

If you live at home and would like to continue to do so as you age, there are some programs you should be aware of that can provide assistance and help to you.

Vial Of Life

Many local sheriff's offices take part in the *Vial of Life* program. The program provides a form you complete with your name, medical conditions, medication, doctor's contact information, and who to contact in an emergency. The information is then placed in an empty pill bottle and attached to the top shelf of the refrigerator. Emergency workers will automatically check for the bottle if there is a call.

> **SENIOR TIP**
>
> Information is available from:
>
> **Vial of Life Project**
> 2 Catamaran Street, Suite 3
> Marina del Rey, CA 90292
> **www.vialoflife.com**

Mail Carrier Alert Program

The *Mail Carrier Alert Program* allows a postal carrier to notify a person's family if a senior does not retrieve his or her mail. Contact your local post office for information and to find out if your local postal carriers participate in the program, since participation varys by zip code.

> **SENIOR TIP**
>
> For more information about the Mail Carrier Alert Program, contact:
>
> **Carrier Alert Program**
> **National Association of Letter Carriers**
> 100 Indiana Avenue, NW
> Washington, DC 20001-2144
> 202-393-4695
> **www.nalc.org/commun/alert**

Other Programs

Your neighborhood may have a *Phone Assistance League,* which will make daily calls to seniors and will contact family members if there is a problem or no answer. Seniors who can afford to may wish to consider an *emergency alert system* for the home. These systems provide a necklace or bracelet with an emergency button. Once it is pushed, the company administering the system will call 911 or a relative, depending on what kind of response is given by the person wearing it. The systems are available for monthly fees.

–4–

LIFESTYLE

Your social life and home life are important parts of staying active and feeling happy. There are many types of assistance you may qualify for as a senior that can improve your quality of life.

ASSISTANCE WITH MEALS

There are lots of programs that can provide seniors with assistance with food and meals. If you are not sure where to turn or what is available in your area, contact your local agency on aging. This section will help you understand some of the programs available to you.

Food Stamps

Food stamps are available through state nutrition assistance programs. They are not *welfare*. Food stamps provide you with free basic nutritional items, such as milk, yogurt, juice, and peanut butter. Each state has its own nutrition assistance program and will provide food stamps to seniors with qualifying income and assets. Seniors with less than $3000 in liquid assets (your home, car, household goods, and life insurance are not counted towards this amount) are eligible and must meet monthly net income tests. Contact your state

> **SENIOR TIP**
>
> For contact information for your state's food stamp program, visit:
> **www.cbpp.org/8-25-03fa.htm**

department of social services for information about eligibility. If you are homeless or low-income, you may qualify for expedited service, which will give you benefits within five days of application.

Special application procedures allow seniors to apply by mail or by sending an authorized representative (friend or relative) to the office to apply on their behalf. Phone interviews can also be used to determine eligibility. You must provide your Social Security number when applying. Food stamps can be used at all grocery stores and chains and are accepted like cash. You should receive your first stamps within thirty days of application. If your application is denied, tell the food stamp office that you believe it was a mistake. You will then have a hearing scheduled before a hearing officer.

Many seniors do not apply for food stamps because they think the benefit is too small to bother with. In fact, the average benefit for a senior living alone is $45 per month and $112 per month for senior couples. Seniors who live in a facility like a nursing home or assisted-living facility are not eligible.

Meals on Wheels

Meals on Wheels are programs that deliver hot meals to homebound seniors. These programs receive federal funding through the federal *Elderly Nutrition Program* and are available to any senior over age 60. This is not considered an entitlement, even though it is federally funded, so there may be waiting lists in some areas or no participating programs. These programs are important not only because they can provide seniors with hot meals, but also because they bring

SENIOR TIP

Contact **Meals on Wheels** at:

1414 Prince Street, suite 302
Alexandria, VA 22314
703-548-5558
www.mowaa.org

The website has a search feature that allows you to locate a program in your area.

human contact to homebound seniors and offer them a chance to interact with another person. The Meals on Wheels workers can also check up on seniors and determine if they need assistance of any kind.

Senior Farmer's Market Nutrition Program

The *Senior Farmer's Market Nutrition Program* is a federally-funded program that is administered by the states. The program provides coupons to seniors for free food from farmer's markets, roadside stands, and community-supported agriculture programs. To qualify, you must be age 60 or older and have income less than 185% of the federal *poverty income guidelines* (in 2003 this was $16,613 for one or $22,422 for two). The coupons are issued once a year and are valid only during your state's growing season. Not all markets accept them, so it is best to get a list of participating markets from your state program. Contact your local agency on aging for information.

Currently, 35 states offer this program. The states include:

- Alabama
- Alaska
- Arkansas
- California
- Connecticut
- Florida
- Hawaii
- Illinois
- Indiana
- Kansas
- Kentucky
- Louisiana
- Maine
- Maryland
- Massachusetts
- Minnesota

- Missouri
- Montana
- Nebraska
- New Hampshire
- New Jersey
- New York
- Nevada
- North Carolina
- Ohio
- Oregon
- Pennsylvania
- Rhode Island
- South Carolina
- Tennessee
- Vermont
- Virginia
- Washington
- West Virginia
- Wisconsin

Commodity Supplemental Food Program

The *commodity supplemental food program* provides a free box of a variety of food once a month to seniors age 60 and up with income at or below 130% of the federal poverty income guidelines. Contact your local agency on aging for application information.

SENIOR TIP

Find the current federal poverty income guidelines online at **www.aoa.gov/prof/poverty_guidelines/poverty_guidelines.asp**

Elderly Nutrition Program

The U.S. Department of Health and Human Services' Administration on Aging provides funding for senior meals. Part of this funding goes to Meals on Wheels for homebound seniors, but other funding goes to what are called *congregate meals*—meals served in places where seniors can go, such as senior centers, churches, schools, and other community facilities. All food served for seniors at these locations is free, however, there may be waiting lists or lack of available facilities in your area.

UTILITY ASSISTANCE

The *Energy Assistance Program* is a federally-funded program which helps pay heating costs. If you receive SSI, you are probably eligible. For more information, contact **www.acf.dhhs.gov/programs/liheap**.

Link Up America

If you do not have a telephone or cannot afford the bills you have, you may be eligible for assistance provided by local phone companies through *Link Up America*. This program reduces you basic charges by 50% if you meet income requirements. See **www.calling-plans.com/fcc/link-up-america.html** for more information.

TRANSPORTATION

Being able to get to places is one of the most important ways to remain independent and feel as if your life is fulfilling. Staying mobile allows you to remain active in your community. There are many options available.

Drivers' Licenses

Your driver's license is a symbol of your independence, however, many states have begun to limit the rights of seniors to drive. Florida drivers over age 79 are now required to pass an eye exam to renew their licenses. Other states require seniors to renew licenses in person; renew them more often; or, take road tests to renew a license.

The following list describes the states that have restrictions on licensing for seniors and what restrictions are in place. The states with restrictions include:

- *Alaska*—no mail renewal over age 69;
- *Arizona*—no mail renewal over age 70, renewal every five years over age 65, vision test verification form required for ages 65 and up;
- *California*—no mail renewal over age 70;
- *Colorado*—no mail renewal over age 66, renewal every five years over age 61;
- *Connecticut*—ages 65 and up can renew by mail if a showing of hardship is demonstrated;
- *District of Columbia*—vision test at or after age 70 is required, reaction test may be required, statement from physician is required certifying physical and mental competency to drive, road and written tests may be required over age 75;
- *Florida*—vision test required after age 79, may be completed at a physician's or optometrist's office;
- *Hawaii*—renewal every two years for ages 72 and up;
- *Idaho*—renewal every four years for ages 63 and up;
- *Illinois*—road test required for ages 75 and up, renewal every two years for ages 81 to 86 and every year after age 87;
- *Indiana*—renewal every three years for ages 75 and up;
- *Iowa*—renewal every two years for ages 70 and up;
- *Kansas*—renewal every four years for ages 65 and up;
- *Louisiana*—no mail renewal for ages 70 and up or to those who renewed by mail the last time;
- *Maine*—vision test required for first renewal after turning 40 and every second renewal between until age 62, yearly vision tests after age 62, renewal every four years for ages 65 and up;

- *Missouri*—renewal every three years for ages 70 and up;
- *Montana*—renewal every four years for ages 75 and up;
- *New Hampshire*—road test required for ages 75 and up;
- *New Mexico*—renewal every four years for ages 75 and up;
- *Oregon*—vision screening required every eight years for ages 50 and up;
- *Rhode Island*—renewal every two years for ages 70 and up;
- *South Carolina*—renewal every five years for ages 65 and up, vision test required for ages 65 and up;
- *Tennessee*—licenses do not expire once you are 65; and,
- *Utah*—vision test required for ages 65 and up.

(States not listed do not have any restrictions on senior drivers at the time this book was written.)

Having some driving difficulties does not necessarily mean you have to give up your license. There are many senior driving rehabilitation courses available that can help senior drivers hone their skills and update their safety precautions.

SENIOR TIP

AAA Foundation for Traffic Safety's Senior website **www.seniordrivers.org** offers information about safety tips and classes for senior drivers.

Assistance with Transportation

Assistance with transportation for health care, shopping, worship, and community access is available through local programs. Often these programs are run by area senior centers and churches, but you can obtain more information through your local agency on aging or through the *Eldercare Locator* at 800-677-1116 or **www.eldercare.gov**.

INCOME TAX RELIEF

You are entitled to a 15% tax reduction if you meet certain income guidelines, you are age 65, or if you are disabled. This reduction will not result in a refund, only in a reduction of the amount you owe. If you are over 65 or are blind, and do not itemize your deductions, you are entitled to an additional standard deduction. If you are both blind and over 65, you can take two additional standard deductions. You may also qualify for the *earned income credit* if you are working and have a child or grandchild living with you. This is a credit that reduces what you owe and may entitle you to a refund.

NOTE: *If your medical expenses are greater than 7.5% of your income, you may be able to deduct them.*

If you sell your home, you can take an exclusion for the profit you earned on the sale of the home. You must have lived in the home for at least two years. Consult your tax advisor for more details about these various tax options.

SENIOR CENTERS

Senior centers are important community-based lifestyle centers for seniors. Senior centers often offer free entertainment, classes, crafts, borrowing libraries, computer access, games, meals, transportation, and services such as flu shots and health-care checks. Senior center activities and programs are free and can provide social contact and community for people who might otherwise be isolated. Contact your local agency on aging to

SENIOR TIP

Seniors are entitled to purchase a $10 lifetime pass to national parks, monuments, and recreation areas. For more information, visit:

www.fs.fed.us

obtain information about your local senior center.

SENIOR TIP

Search **www.seniordiscounts.com** for businesses in your area that offer senior discounts.

SENIOR DISCOUNTS

Senior discounts are an often overlooked benefit available to help seniors cut costs and enjoy life. Many businesses, such as restaurants, movie theaters, and pharmacies, offer discounts to seniors age 55 and older on a daily basis. Some stores and other businesses have special senior discount days when discounts are available to seniors. Additionally, AARP members are entitled to many member discounts. Some stores or businesses issue senior discount cards so you do not have to prove your age each time. Your local senior center may be able to provide you with details on which area businesses offer discounts.

READING

If you experience vision difficulties, large-print books are becoming more widely available. Many public libraries maintain separate large-print sections. *Amazon* has a separate section on its website for large print books. Books on tape are another alternative for those who enjoy reading. Many libraries carry books on tape and they are available in bookstores as well.

SENIOR TIP

Shop for large print books online at:
www.largeprintbooks.com
Read reviews of large-print books at
www.largeprintreviews.com

Many areas also have programs where volunteers will read books, magazines, or newspapers to visually-impaired people. Check with your area agency on aging for information about programs offered in your area.

EMPLOYMENT

Continuing to work is an important right for many seniors. Laws against age discrimination in employment do exist, but there are some allowable mandatory retirement situations. (See Chapter 10 for more information.) Many seniors are interested in finding other work after retirement.

Assistance

The federal *Senior Community Service Employment Program* provides part-time employment and training opportunities to low-income seniors age 55 and up. The program places seniors in government and community agencies and pays minimum wage, but offers training and the opportunity to move to other higher-paying positions.

For more information, contact:

U.S. Department of Labor
Employment and Training Administration
Division of Older Worker Programs
200 Constitution Avenue NW, Room N-4641
Washington, DC 20210
877-US-2JOBS
http://wdsc.doleta.gov/seniors

AARP SCSEP National Office
601 E Street NW
Washington DC 20049
202-434-2020
www.aarp.org/scsep-locate (to locate a local office)

Senior-Friendly Employers

Many employers have become more senior-friendly in recent years. You may have seen commercials from well-known companies such as *McDonald's* and *Wal-Mart* featuring senior employees. Finding a senior-friendly employer can be difficult. AARP publishes a yearly list of fifty employers they determine to be the best employers for seniors.

SENIOR TIP

Read the current list of AARP's best employers for seniors at **www.aarp.org/bestemployers**

Social Security Benefits

Some seniors feel that laws discourage them from working once they begin to collect social security benefits. The law actually only affects some seniors. Your benefits are only affected until you reach the full retirement age of 65 and two months. If you begin receiving benefits before full retirement age, for every $2 you earn above the income limit (which was $11,520 in 2003), you lose $1 in benefits. In the year you will reach full retirement age, you lose $1 in benefits for every $3 you earn over the income limit for this group (which was $30,720 in 2003) in the months before you reach the full retirement age. Once you are 65 and two months, you can earn anything you want and will lose no benefits at all. For the purposes of this rule, only your salary (or your net as a self-employed person) will count as earnings and this does not include benefits. There is one small exception to the rule. In the year you retire, you will receive your full benefits without any deductions for the months you are retired in that year.

VOLUNTEERING

Many seniors find that volunteering provides them with the opportunity to stay busy, do good, and feel a sense of satisfaction about their lives. The *Senior Corps* is a federal program designed to help seniors locate volunteer opportunities. There are three main components to the program: foster grandparents, senior companions, and the retired and senior volunteer program (RSVP). The programs involve seniors in a wide range of activities, with a wide range of people. For more information, contact:

Senior Corps
1201 New York Avenue, NW
Washington, DC 20525
202-606-5000
www.fs.fed.us

–5–

HOUSING

How happy and fulfilling your life is can be affected by many factors, including where you live. Many seniors want to understand what their future housing options are, since age and health problems can necessitate changes in living arrangements. There are many options, choices, and possibilities to consider, but perhaps the most important thing to understand is that you have the right to choose where you live. Despite complications with insurance, Medicaid, or Medicare, the bottom line is that the choice about where you live is one that only you can make. This chapter explains your housing options and what your rights are in each type of location.

LIVING AT HOME

Whether you remain in your own home or move in with a family member, living at home can provide the most independence and is often the option most people prefer. Remaining at home is quite feasible for many older seniors, as long as there is assistance. Consider these types of assistance that may help make staying at home possible:

- food deliveries by Meals on Wheels (see Chapter 4 for more information);
- home repair, cleaning, and lawn care by family members or hired professionals;
- help bringing in the mail or paper and assistance with snow removal by neighbors or family;

- medical alert systems to summon help if ever needed; and,
- transportation by friends, family, or local senior centers.

(See Chapter 6 for information about making your home safe and accessible.)

MOBILE HOMES

Forty-one percent of trailer homes are owned by seniors. Trailer or manufactured homes can present an affordable alternative to home ownership, while providing a one-story living space that is often just the right size for a senior or a senior couple who want independence but not a huge house.

Most manufactured homes are purchased in an existing mobile home park (although you can consider buying a trailer and placing it on land you or a family member own.) When you purchase a manufactured home, you usually buy the home, but rent the land that it is on. The land is typically owned by the owner of the park or community. Many states have a mobile home owner's bill of rights—laws that set out exactly what your park owner can and cannot do and what your rights are in a mobile home park. For more information about this contact your state attorney general's office.

It is important to remember that you are the owner of the home and the park owner cannot enter your home without permission (except in an emergency), evict you without proper notice, or create rules that are unreasonable. The park owner is the landlord for the land, but you are the owner of the actual structure.

RENTALS

Many seniors find that renting an apartment suits their needs better than owning a home and having to deal with the upkeep home ownership requires.

If you live in a rental, you can make modifications to the property to fit your needs. The federal *Fair Housing Act* requires landlords to permit tenants to make changes to the unit if they have a medical or physical condition that requires it. This can include things such as adding handrails or lowering sinks to become wheelchair accessible.

Landlords may not discriminate against you because of your age under the *Fair Housing Act*. This means that they cannot charge you more rent than comparable tenants, place additional requirements on you, or refuse to rent to you because of your age. Additionally, landlords cannot discriminate against you if you have a disability. If you believe that you are being discriminated against, contact your state's attorney general's office or contact your local Department of Housing and Urban Development (HUD) office to file a complaint. (See Appendix A for contact information.)

IN-HOME CARE

Health care is something that prevents many seniors from remaining independent. It is possible to remain in your home and get the health care you need by hiring in-home, health-care workers.

When choosing home-health workers, you may have a lot of choices or very few, depending on where you live and the number of agencies in your area. When you do have choices, think carefully about the people you consider. Are they pleasant, kind, gentle, and patient? Are they competent? Are they bonded (insured so that any damage they cause is covered) or trustworthy enough so that you feel bonding is not necessary?

Remember that the more skilled the provider, the more expensive the care. A *registered nurse* (RN) will cost much more than an

SENIOR TIP

For information and support contact:

National Association for Home Care
228 Seventh Street, SE
Washington, DC 20003
(202) 547-7424
www.nahc.org

aide, so make sure you match needs to qualifications—closely. Many people feel that it makes more financial sense to enter a senior residence than to pay for in-home care.

Actually, it is less expensive for most seniors to remain at home, if they can afford the out-of-pocket costs involved. Medicaid and Medicare do not pay much of these costs. Expect home care to start at about $10 an hour for basic housekeeping assistance and top out near $100 an hour for the most skilled nursing care.

If you hire in-home health providers but do not do so through an agency, you are supposed to treat the providers like employees and withhold taxes and provide W-2s. Many nurses and aides do home care part-time when they are not working for a hospital or facility and are willing to work *off-the-books*. Be aware that you are legally required to withhold taxes. Discuss this with an accountant.

NOTE: *Hiring an in-home health provider through can agency alleviates your responsibility to withhold taxes.*

When selecting home health-care workers, you need to narrow down exactly what kind of care or assistance is needed so that you know who you need to hire. There are several choices, which include the following.

- *Registered Nurses (RN)*. This is the most expensive choice. Depending on the level of care needed, you may be able to arrange for an RN visit once per day or once per week. They can perform a full range of medical care and administer medications. They also are valuable because they can call your physician and request medication changes or get clarifications on certain types of treatment.
- *Licensed Practical Nurses (LPN)*. Licensed practical nurses are trained nurses who are not authorized to perform as many medical services as RNs, but can monitor blood pressure and do other medical tasks, such as managing IVs.

- *Aides.* For the performance of personal hygiene care and some noninvasive medical care, an aide may be your best choice. Often an aide will do light housekeeping and prepare meals. They can be certified or uncertified (licensed or unlicensed by the state).
- *Therapists.* Therapists can be one of the many types of licensed providers who assist patients in rehabilitating or improving physical abilities.
- *Housekeepers.* Housekeeping care can be provided by any unlicensed worker who performs household tasks. If a little extra help around the house, instead of medical care, is what you need, a housekeeper may be the best option.
- *Home Health-Care Agencies.* Many types of home care can be obtained from agencies that employ home health-care workers and provide you with the staff you need. You pay the agency directly and often have little say over who takes the shifts. However, all staff is bonded and there is a large selection of workers, so if one worker calls in sick, there is another one to replace him or her. Make sure the agency is Medicare/Medicaid certified so that the care will be covered. Get the Medicare survey report about the agency from your state department of health to evaluate the agency.

Ask these questions when evaluating home care agencies.

- How long have you been providing services?
- How are employees selected and trained?
- Do nurses or therapists evaluate the patient's care and progress?
- Is the family included in the plan of care?
- Is the plan of care carefully and completely documented?
- Do supervisors oversee the care that is provided?
- Are written statements of costs provided?

- What kind of procedures are in place to deal with emergencies?
- How is HIPAA privacy ensured?

Payment for Home Care

Medicare will pay for up to thirty-five hours of in-home, health-care per week if:

- a doctor certifies it is medically necessary and sets up a plan of care;
- part-time skilled nursing care, physical therapy and/or speech therapy are needed;
- the patient is homebound; and,
- the services are provided by a Medicare certified agency.

Coverage includes nursing, physical therapy, social services, aides, and medical supplies, but only covers "reasonable" costs. Anything over what Medicare considers reasonable is paid out-of-pocket. Full-time skilled nursing care, meals delivered to the home, and homemaker services are not covered.

Medicaid will also cover some home health-care services. Check with your local agency on aging for details on what your state's plan covers.

NOTE: *Because Medicaid pay is low, many agencies will not accept Medicaid.*

A private insurance policy may also provide some coverage for in-home health care. Check with your carrier.

SELF-PROVIDED CARE

If you have a spouse who needs care, you or other family members may be able to provide some of that care. You can learn to perform finger sticks for diabetes, colostomy bag care, and other routine procedures.

A nurse or aide can teach you or other family members how to monitor certain conditions, change bandages, and assist with walking and bathing. It can be helpful to have a professional, such as an RN, come in once a day or once every few days (depending on the medical situation) to answer questions and provide guidance. Providing medical care yourself requires a great time commitment and it is best to arrange times when others can assist you or give you a break.

SNOWBIRDS

Many seniors hear the siren call of warm climates. Going south for the winter can be a way to stay active and avoid many winter illnesses, such as colds and flu.

If you do decide to head to a warmer climate for part of the year, make sure you have a plan in place for caring for both homes when you are absent from them. Perhaps a neighbor can keep an eye on things or a family member can check on the home once in a while.

You will have options in terms of your official residence. You can maintain the northern state as your official state of residence or you can decide that you will spend more time in the south and change your residence to that state. The state you are a resident of is the place where you will renew your driver's license, file your income taxes, vote (contact your board of elections for an absentee ballot if you will be out of the state on election day), and apply for Medicaid or Medicare. You can register vehicles in either state. You will pay property taxes to the states where you own real estate.

When receiving medical care in the nonresident state, you will need to take some extra steps to be sure your care is covered by your insurance plan, Medicaid, or Medicare. Medicaid will have an out-of-state care coordinator who will handle payment issues for your care. It may take some extra steps to get a provider in another state to accept payment from your Medicaid program, which can involve paperwork and phone calls. Keep good records of what is approved and follow up with your provider (to check on payment) and with your out-of-state care coordinator frequently. When using private insurance, be aware that you may have to pay higher co-pays or co-insurance costs when you obtain out-of-network care.

APARTMENT LIFE

Many seniors choose to sell their homes and rent a home. If you choose to do so, remember that you are entering into a landlord tenant relationship with the owner. Your rights against housing discrimination are described in Chapter 10.

Lease

When you rent an apartment, you will sign a lease or contract with the landlord. If you have nothing in writing, then you are a month-to-month tenant (which means that at the end of each month you or the landlord can choose to give one month's notice and end the tenancy.)

Security Deposit

The landlord can request a security deposit from you, which is usually equal to one month's rent. This money is held in escrow by the landlord against any damage you might do while living there. It is returned to you when you leave if there is no damage.

Landlord Tenant Relationship

As the tenant, you must pay your rent on time and keep the premises in good condition during your rental period. The landlord is responsible for all repairs to the unit and for keeping it safe and in compliance with all local building codes. (Check with your town or city for information about your local laws.)

Rental Assistance

You are eligible for Section 8 housing assistance if you are over age 62 or are disabled and meet your local income requirements. If you are certified, you have sixty days to find an apartment.

Once you sign a lease, the local branch of the *Department of Housing and Urban Development* (HUD) inspects it to make sure it meets federal standards. If it does, the agency signs a contract with your landlord agreeing to pay part of the rent on your behalf. You will pay the rest of the rent that is not covered by the agency. The tenant pays no more than 30% of his income.

RV LIFE

Many seniors decide to hit the road in a *recreational vehicle* (RV) for an extended period of time. A life on the road can be exciting, but you will want to make sure you have a plan in place to make life simpler.

Arrange to have your mail sent to a post office box so you can pick it up or consider forwarding it to a family member's home so he or she can alert you if something important is delivered. You may wish to set up an account with a bank that has branches throughout the country, so that you can easily deposit and withdraw funds. Arrange to have as many things as possible deposited electronically and paid automatically from your account. Plan to make regular trips to one geographical area so that you can have a primary care physician who knows you and is familiar with your medical needs. Always carry your medical file with you on your travels, so that you have current medical information you can provide should you become ill.

Internet

The Internet will allow you to email friends and family, pay bills, and transfer money between accounts. You can use a laptop with wireless internet access using a cell phone line while on the road. Some RV parks have recreation centers with broadband Internet access or you can go to a local public library to use the Internet for free.

LIVING WITH FAMILY

Moving in with a family member can be a good alternative to senior living or assisted living. When you live with a family member, your living costs are usually very low. You have the comfort of being in familiar surroundings with people you know and love.

However, living with family is not always the perfect situation. Arguments can be intense and it can be difficult to give up your independence and live under someone else's roof. It can also be difficult to know when a move should take place to a senior residence and hard to make that decision. If you do move in with a family member, talk about what items you will be able to bring with you and where they will go. Discuss what room or rooms will be yours. Try to get a sense of the routine in the household and understand that it will take some time for everyone involved to adjust to the change. If you will be contributing to the household expenses and bills, make sure you reach a firm agreement about how you will share expenses and what your responsibilities will be.

SENIOR LIVING

Senior-living residences are also referred to as *independent living* or *senior apartments*. These are apartments or townhomes designated especially for seniors. Some can be very resort-like, while lower-end facilities are like small apartments. They offer the least restrictive type of away from home arrangement. Residents live in an apartment by themselves or with a spouse. Each unit contains—at the very least—a cooking area, living area, sleeping area, and bathroom so that the resident can live independently. Most senior living units are handicap accessible and outfitted to provide conveniences that make the unit senior friendly. There are usually common areas, such as activity rooms, where residents can socialize with each other. There may also be additional facilities such as pools or golf courses. Organized activities and outings are planned by the facility. Senior living is an excellent choice for those who cannot remain at home, but do not need ongoing medical care or assistance.

Senior living units have some staff on the premises, but staff may not be available 24 hours a day. Most senior living units have call buttons or emergency pull cords to contact staff, a local hospital, or a nursing home should assistance be needed.

Senior living is appropriate for seniors who are mobile, require little assistance, and are able to cook and handle personal care for themselves. Senior living offers the freedom of independence with the reassurance of knowing that assistance is close at hand should it be needed. It provides freedom from home maintenance and offers a feeling of community, since residents spend time together and can ease loneliness through group interaction.

There are usually no services included in the price of a senior living unit, but services can be arranged at extra costs. Cleaning services, personal care aides, meal preparation, visits by registered nurses, and other types of assistance can normally be provided at extra cost if requested.

Costs

Seniors in residences normally pay a monthly rent. Some residences may adjust the rent with regard to income. There is no state or federal financial assistance available for senior-living rent. It is not covered by Medicaid, Medicare, or private insurance.

Finding a Senior Residence

Contact your local agency on aging for a list of senior residences in your area (see Appendix D.) You may know friends or relatives who live in senior housing. If so, ask them about the place they live and visit them there. You can also use your local phone book to compile a list of nearby senior residences.

Once you have a list of residences you are interested in, look at them online or ask them to mail you information. Then make appointments to go visit them. It is a good idea to bring a family member or friend with you to help you evaluate the place. Be sure to get a brochure from each place to help you remember and compare them. Get the costs in writing. It may be a good idea to take notes while speaking with the staff since, there will be many details explained and it will be impossible to remember them all.

When talking with the staff or sales representative, be sure to ask the following questions.

- What are the costs?
- What do the costs include?
- Are there application fees?
- Are other services available at additional cost?
- Do residents have to meet mobility or physical ability minimums?
- How long do you have to relocate once you no longer meet the minimums?
- Is staff available 24 hours a day?
- Are call buttons or cords part of the units and if so, who do they call?
- What kinds of activities are planned and how often?
- What kinds of outings are planned and how often?
- Are there extra costs for group activities?
- Where are the common areas?
- Are outer doors and gates locked at night?
- How many residents do you have?
- How many openings do you have?
- Is there a waiting list and if so, how long is it?
- Is rent adjusted according to income?
- What kind of proof of income is required?
- Are overnight guests (including children) permitted?
- Are pets permitted?
- Are furnishings included and if so, what?
- What kinds of decorative changes can residents make to their units?

- What kind of security is in place?
- Is transportation offered and is there a fee?
- Do staff members regularly check in on residents?

When touring the facility, there are things to look for that will help you get a feel for a particular place. Some of the things you should look for include the following.

- Are the common areas clean and comfortable?
- Do residents interact with each other?
- Are activities posted and if so, do they look interesting and frequent enough?
- Are you shown a resident unit?
- Are common areas clean and pleasant?
- Are the units bright and comfortable?
- Are home safety measures evident? (See Chapter 6 for a list.)
- Are the hallways brightly lit?
- Do residents seem happy and friendly?
- Are call buttons or cords evident?
- Are staff members friendly and helpful?
- Are the room sizes adequate?
- Does the place smell pleasant?
- Are exits clearly marked?
- Is everything handicap accessible?
- Can you see yourself living here and being happy?

Evaluating the Facility

Plan to make an unscheduled visit so that you can see what the residence looks like when the staff does not know you are coming. Once you have done this, you need to evaluate what you have seen and compare the different residences you have visited. You will want to weigh cost against comfort. Consider the services and activities available at each residence, and think about what services you currently need and those you anticipate possibly needing in the future. Think about the types of people you saw living there. You may also want to weigh in the distance to relatives' or friends' homes.

Evaluating the Contract

The senior residence facility will have a written agreement between itself and the residents. When evaluating the contract, make sure that the monthly fee and the fees for extra services are clearly laid out. Be aware of restrictions on visitors and guests, indications that fees may rise without warning, and provisions that allow the residence to evict you without cause. Find out if there is an application fee or an up-front initiation fee, and if so, whether or not they are refundable.

Make sure that any services you have been promised are listed in writing. Check to see if the contract guarantees you a specific unit and if the residence has the right to require you to move to a different unit at any point. Only the senior moving into the residence should sign the contract. (Other family members do not need to sign.)

Dealing with Problems

Because senior living is not medical care, it is not regulated by the state. You are essentially a tenant and the facility is your landlord. If you have problems with the services you were promised, you must turn to your contract. If those services are contained in the contract, you or a family member should approach the management and explain that they are legally obligated to provide the things contained in the contract.

Small claims court is the option to pursue if the facility does not live up to the contract. You can use an attorney to represent you in small claims court or you can represent yourself. Additionally, many municipalities have housing court, where landlord/tenant problems are heard. Contact your town or city for information on the type of court available for your housing dispute. Since you are a tenant and not an owner, the facility is responsible for all maintenance to your unit.

ADULT DAY CARE

Adult day care is a growing option for many seniors and is usually appropriate for seniors who live with a spouse or family member and need care during the day while family members are at work or otherwise occupied. Most centers are open for eight to ten hours during week days and some may also offer weekend care. Some centers specialize in Alzheimer's disease or dementia patients, so be sure to ask what types of seniors they accept. Care centers provide meals, activities, assistance with daily living, recreation, exercise and more, in a safe environment. Day care is not covered by Medicare, but most offer sliding scale fees and may also have some state or county funding. There is some coverage for day care and transportation by Medicaid.

ASSISTED LIVING

Assisted-living facilities, also called *custodial-care facilities, domiciliary care facilities, sheltered housing, residential-care facilities,* or *intermediate care facilities,* are designed for seniors who need help with the activities of daily life. These needs can range from meal preparation and bathing to medication management. Assisted living allows seniors who do not need extensive medical or health care, to remain independent, yet receive the assistance they need to function and remain safe.

Assisted living facilities usually offer one room or small apartment units where a senior can live and receive assistance from a staff for a variety of everyday needs. Sometimes these facilities are in converted buildings, new buildings, or large residences. Rooms are normally furnished, but some facilities permit residents to bring their own furnishings.

The types of services that are available vary from place to place but usually include help with dressing, bathing, housekeeping, laundry, transportation, and medications. Meals are usually offered in a group setting. Residents are monitored occasionally throughout the day. Social activities are an important part of the services offered, as is the twenty-four hour staff.

Assisted-living facilities will accept couples as well as individuals and can be a good choice for any senior who just cannot continue to manage at home or in a senior living residence. Pets are usually not permitted and overnight guests are not allowed. It is important to understand that residents are not trapped there. They can go on group outings, to family functions, and so on. Assisted living is just a place to live, not a life sentence.

Cost

Most assisted-living facilities cost around $1200 to $2000 per month, but many can cost much more. Most states allow for Medicaid coverage for assisted living, but Medicare does not offer any coverage. Long-term care insurance policies may provide coverage. Check with your carrier for information.

Finding a Place

Start with facilities where friends or family live or have lived. Ask friends, neighbors, and colleagues for experience they have had with these types of facilities. Contact your local agency on aging for a list of local care facilities. Once you have a list of places you would like to consider, look at them online or ask for information by mail, then call to set up appointments. If you are in need of assisted living, it is likely that a friend or family member will have to do most of the legwork for you, although you should play a large part in making the decision if you can.

When gathering information about a facility, there are many questions you should ask. Some of those questions should include the following.

- What are the costs and what do they include?
- What are the fees for additional services?

- What is the staff-to-resident ratio?
- Do a resident's personal items need to be labeled?
- Is there a fee for laundry services?
- How often are rooms cleaned?
- How are medications dispensed?
- What types of activities are planned and how often?
- Are there residents with dementia or Alzheimer's disease?
- What kind of security is in place?
- Are friends and family encouraged to visit?
- How large are the rooms?
- How often are beds and linens changed?
- What items can residents bring with them?
- Are choices available for meals or is only one entrée prepared?
- What kind of transportation is available for outings or doctor appointments?
- How often is transportation available?
- What kind of medical care is available on the premises?
- Is a physical exam or assessment required before admission?
- Are there minimum physical ability requirements residents must meet?
- Are single and double rooms available?

Once your questions have been answered, you still need to listen to what your instincts are telling you about a particular facility. Some of the personal indicators you should take note of include:

- a homey atmosphere that is not institutional;
- a facility that does not feel too large;
- clean bathrooms;
- no odors;
- a friendly staff;
- a floor plan that is not confusing;
- good lighting;

- nonskid floors;
- handicap accessibility;
- handrails in the halls;
- clearly marked exits;
- a place residents can go for solitude;
- an outdoor area, patio, or courtyard;
- mobile, active residents;
- emergency call systems in the rooms;
- happy residents;
- lists of activities for residents;
- visiting family and friends;
- community rooms, activity rooms, and living rooms; and,
- security.

Evaluating

After you (or your family and friends) have asked questions and looked around, come back unannounced at another time. Try to visit unannounced during the day and at night to see how the facility is run during both times. You may also wish to eat a meal or two at the facility to evaluate the food. Consider how convenient the facility is to family, friends, senior centers, and churches. Decide if you feel the facility is clean and residents are treated well.

> **SENIOR TIP**
>
> You can read a sample assisted-living contract online at:
>
> **www.aahsa.org/public/residentcontract.doc**
>
> (Note that a window will come up asking for an authentication number. Press cancel and you will be taken to the document.)

Contracts

Once you select an assisted-living facility, you will be asked to sign a contract. Only you will be signing this document. Family members should never sign a contract for a senior's care unless they do so using your power of attorney. If they sign, it will make them financially responsible for the fees.

Make sure the contract clearly states the rates and the costs of any optional services. The contract should state that the facility will provide care for you as long as it is able to meet your care needs. Make sure that the facility has the right to require you to leave only for the following reasons:

- nonpayment;
- if it is unable to meet your needs;
- if you become a danger to yourself or other residents; or,
- if the facility closes.

Never sign a contract that releases the facility from all liability for harm to you or your belongings.

NURSING HOMES

If you need should nursing home care, you will likely be too ill to make the choice yourself and will need to rely on family or friends to find a place for you. However, knowing now what to look for can help your family or friends be prepared in advance. This also provides an opportunity for you to talk with them about what your wishes are and to think about what kinds of choices you want them to help you make should it ever be necessary.

Nursing homes are also sometimes called long-term care facilities or skilled-nursing facilities. Whatever their name, these facilities provide nursing and medical care for patients in a residential setting. It is important to realize that nursing home care does not have to be the *end of the line*. Often people need to have short-term stays in nursing homes after hospitalizations or for rehabilitative purposes. Other patients do require constant long-term care and for this they do need to become permanent nursing home residents. If you need nursing home care, you most likely will be told by your health-care provider, hospital discharge planner, or assisted living staff member.

It is important to ask questions about exactly what kind of care is needed and whether it is possible to get this kind of care at home.

Costs

Medicare will pay for nursing-home stays for only thirty days, with a total 100-day-maximum after a three-day hospital stay. Coverage exists only as long as the patient needs skilled nursing care. If you qualify for Medicaid, Medicaid will pay the costs of nursing home care once Medicare coverage ends. Nursing homes are not required to accept Medicare or Medicaid. If a nursing home does accept Medicaid, it can limit the number of beds available for Medicaid residents. Thus, if the cost of your care will be covered by Medicaid, you may not be able to get into a facility if all the Medicaid beds are full. However, if a patient enters as private pay or Medicare pay and then becomes Medicaid pay (by spending down to Medicaid), the nursing home cannot make him or her leave and must accept Medicaid if they have other patients with Medicaid.

A facility that does not accept Medicaid will not be required to keep this kind of patient and can require private payment. A patient who enters a nursing home under Medicare or Medicaid cannot be required to pay a security deposit or advance payment. Also, if a facility accepts Medicaid, it will have a set number of days Medicaid will pay for the bed to be held while the patient is away at a hospital or other facility. This is called the facility's *bedhold policy*.

Nursing homes are expensive, and according to the AARP (formerly known as the American Association of Retired Persons), the average cost per year is about $50,000. If you have long-term care insurance or private insurance, some of the costs may be covered. You need to read the insurance policy closely to understand what is covered, since you cannot assume the policy will provide complete coverage. Many have caps or percentages that apply to payment.

NOTE: *Nursing homes cannot require a family member to guarantee payment.*

> **SENIOR TIP**
>
> The Eldercare Locator is a free national directory that can help you find care in your area. You can reach them at 800-677-1116 or **www.eldercare.gov/Eldercare/Public/Home.asp**

Finding a Nursing Home

Learn about the nursing homes in your area. Talk with friends and family members about their impressions of local facilities. Ask your doctor for information and advice. If you are in a hospital, talk with (and have family or friends talk with) hospital social workers and discharge planners. Your local agency on aging can provide you with a list of area nursing homes. You may also want to contact your *long-term care ombudsman*. Ombudsmen are state employees who evaluate and inspect nursing homes. (A list of ombudsmen is in Appendix D.)

Nursing homes are governed by the *Nursing Home Reform Act*, which contains standards for nursing homes to follow. (see Appendix E.)

Once you, your family, or your friends have created a list of nursing homes to consider, your family or friends should make appointments to speak to an administrator and to get a tour of the facility. They should plan on returning unannounced once during the day and once in the evening so they can see what the facility is like at all times of day.

Some of the questions they will need to ask the nursing home administrator include the following.

- What are the costs?
- Are there extra fees?
- Is Medicaid accepted?

- How many Medicaid beds are there and how many are available?
- What is the employee-to-resident ratio?
- Are there separate areas for patients with dementia and Alzheimer's disease?
- What is the daily schedule?
- How many RNs are on duty at a time?
- What is the ratio of RNs to other staff?
- How many patients do they have in total?
- Are activities planned for residents?
- Is there a family and/or resident council?
- Are single rooms available?
- Are there set visiting hours?
- What items may patients bring with them?
- What kind of security is in place?
- What is the bedhold policy?

When your family or friends meet with the administrator, they should ask to see the three most recent state *surveys* (also called *inspections*) of the facility. Your local ombudsman can also help them obtain these and can help them interpret the results. These surveys will help you understand what kinds of problems exist at the facility. Be wary if you see the same problems year after year. A good nursing home will make improvements based on the survey. All nursing homes will have some problems. The purpose of the report is to pinpoint problems so they can be fixed, not to praise facilities for the good work they do.

Staff

There are certain members of the nursing home staff you should be familiar with. The following list includes the people you need to know about and their typical job descriptions.

- Administrative staff—handles paperwork and finances and includes *Administrator, Director of Admissions, Director of Personnel,* and *Finance Director.*
- Medical Director—responsible for overseeing medical care for all residents.
- Nursing Staff—includes *Director of Nursing, Licensed Practical Nurses* (LPNs), *Registered Nurses* (RNs), and nursing assistants or aides.
- Therapists—occupational, physical, recreational and speech therapists.
- Social Services Staff—help residents deal with emotional and social issues.
- Activities Director—manages recreational activities.
- Dietary Staff—handles nutritional needs. The *Food Service Manager* is in charge and dietary assistants prepare meals.

Evaluating the Facility

In general, you want to be sure that residents are treated with kindness and respect, that the facility is clean and cheerful, that the food is appetizing and has variety, that the staff is available and friendly, that residents seem well cared for (talk to some to find out), and that the place is as homey as possible and does not feel like a cold institution.

Warning signs include restraints used on the residents, unpleasant odors, residents' calls for assistance being ignored or put off, listless residents, a lack of privacy, and secrecy by the staff. Make sure you note handicapped access and clear markings on exits. (See the *Nursing Home Checklist* in Appendix F for more pointers.)

When evaluating a nursing home, you have to remember that its primary purpose is to provide medical and daily living care. A person who needs to be in a nursing home is going to have reduced privacy and reduced independence. Find out if your doctor(s) will visit at the nursing home if needed or if you will have to use the providers who work on staff there. Consider how convenient the nursing home is for family members. Look to see if a nursing home resident's bill of rights is posted. Read it and ask for a copy of it.

Understanding the Contract

When you enter a nursing home, you must sign a contract with the facility. It is important to read the contract closely and to do so *before* the day of admission. The contract sets out all of your costs and all of the nursing home's responsibilities. You (or your family members or friends who are helping you with the transition) need to read and understand it. If you were promised something that is not in the contract, you need to insist that it be added in writing. The contract should include information about:

- the basic daily or monthly charge and what it covers (optional services should have pricing listed as well);
- additional charges;
- your right to apply for Medicare or Medicaid;
- when, how, and why you can be transferred to a different room at the home;
- any special diets you may need;
- refund policy;
- bedhold policy; and,
- reasons for discharge.

You are the one who will be signing the documents. Your family members will only be signing if they have power of attorney for you. Sometimes the nursing home might tell family they need to sign as a guarantor or to indicate that they are next of kin or the responsible person to contact. This is unnecessary and they should not sign unless they are willing to take on financial responsibility for your bills.

The *Nursing Home Reform Act* is a federal law that governs nursing homes. The law lists some things that may not be included in a nursing home admission contract. A copy of this law is included in Appendix E. One of the important things included in the law is a restriction on discharges from the home. You can only be made to leave if:

- it is necessary for your welfare because the facility cannot meet your needs;
- your health improves so that you no longer needs to remain there;
- you endanger the safety or health of other residents;
- you do not pay; or,
- the home closes.

Make sure the contract explains its bedhold policy. If you have to temporarily leave the nursing home (for example, for a hospital stay) the facility can charge a fee to hold your bed until you return.

Be on the alert for contracts that:

- limit the home's liability for damage or theft of your belongings;
- require that the resident give all of his or her income to the facility directly;
- have restricted visiting hours;
- require a consent form for unneeded medical procedures as a *precaution;*
- require a living will or health care proxy; or,
- require you to pay even though you are eligible for Medicaid.

NOTE: *Be aware that the facility is always responsible for* negligence *(failing to use appropriate care to prevent harm) no matter what you sign. Some contracts may contain provisions asking you to limit their liability or to waive the right to sue. Do not sign these types of contracts.*

Plan of Care

A nursing home must assess a new patient within fourteen days of admission. Assessments must be redone once a year after that or when any significant change in the patient's health occurs. After an assessment, a *plan of care* must be developed that specifies how the nursing home plans to treat the patient. It is important for the patient and family members to get a copy of this plan and understand it. If you do not agree with something in the plan, say so.

Staff and Facilities

Nursing homes must have twenty-four hour staffing. A registered nurse must be present at least once a day. If there are more than 120 beds, there must be a staff social worker. Dental care, as well as medical care, must be provided to patients. Residents are free to choose their own doctors.

NOTE: *Be aware that the staff that will have the most contact with you will be aides who will handle personal care, meal assistance, and minor medical care.*

There can be no more than four beds per room and each room must have a bathroom accessible with bathing facilities. There must be a system in place for residents to summon assistance. Restraints (physical or drug induced) are not permitted as a general policy, but are allowed by individual order when necessary.

Nursing homes have a board of trustees, who set the overall policies of the facility. The administrative staff handles the day-to day-operations. In addition to nurses and aides, there are therapists, activity coordinators, dieticians, physical therapists, volunteers, and pastoral staff.

For information about problems that occur while living in a nursing home, see Chapter 6.

HOSPICE

Hospice or *palliative care* is a type of in-home or residential care for patients with life-ending illnesses. Hospice care seeks to support the patient and family through this difficult time while keeping the patient comfortable and managing his or her pain. Hospice care is patient and family oriented and uses a different approach than traditional medical care.

The goal of hospice care is to provide a pain-free and dignified death, while minimizing symptoms of the illness. Hospice care does not try to extend or shorten life. Instead, it attempts to make what is left of life pleasant and livable. Most hospices are not in favor of life support systems, feeding tubes, aggressive treatments, or other care designed to prolong life.

Hospice care is designed for patients who have six or fewer months to live. You must be referred to hospice by a doctor for it to be covered by insurance. Once a referral is made, most hospice programs are able to make contact with the patient and family within one day and can begin to provide a full range of services within one week.

Payment

Private insurance and Medicaid cover hospice care. Medicare offers some coverage. To be eligible for Medicare coverage, a patient must receive Medicare Part A (see Chapter 2 for more information about Medicare) and be certified as terminally ill with six or fewer months to live.

Care must be provided by a Medicare-approved hospice. The coverage includes medical staff care, medication, brief hospital stays, in-home health aides, social workers, and family therapists. While receiving hospice care, the patient cannot receive treatment for the disease. So if a person has cancer and is receiving hospice care, he or she cannot receive chemotherapy or radiation—anything designed to treat the disease *instead* of the pain.

Care at Home

Hospice programs were originally created to allow patients to die at home, in comfort, with their family present. Hospice still mainly provides in-home care. Hospice workers visit the home on a regular basis, and immediate support and advice is available by phone. Hospice programs maintain relationships with hospitals so that a patient who needs temporary hospital care can be transferred to a hospital and then returned home while under hospice care.

SENIOR TIP

Contact the National Hospice and Palliative Care Organization at 800-658-8898 or online at **www.nhpco.org** for a list of hospices in your area.

Care at Facilities

Hospice programs have expanded and now usually can provide care at a nursing home, hospital, or other facility. Some hospices maintain their own residential facilities for patients who cannot be cared for at home.

Team Members

Hospice works on a team-based approach to care. A family member is designated as the team leader and works with doctors, nurses, aides, therapists, dieticians, social workers, counselors, and other health-care workers to provide well-rounded care and support.

Family Support

Hospice workers seek to care for the patient *and* the family as one unit. Hospice care does not end with the death of the patient. Bereavement counseling is provided for at least one year after the death. Hospice programs also offer respite care, allowing family caregivers free time while the patient is cared for by other team members.

Evaluating Programs

There may be several hospice programs in your area, so you may have options from which to choose. Ask if the agency is certified (important because Medicare will not pay for the care if the agency is not certified), what the staffs' credentials are, and how long they have been in existence. Also determine how many staff member are on a team, what their admission requirements are, where they provide care, and how they plan to care for you.

Making the Decision

Making the decision to obtain hospice care can be a difficult one because it is an admission that the end of life is near. For a doctor to recommend hospice care, he or she must believe that the patient's life is ending and that there is not much traditional medicine can offer to cure, hold back, or stop the illness.

Coming to this decision can be very emotional and painful, but it often brings a sense of relief. Hospice care offers many patients the opportunity to relax and enjoy the days that remain without the stress of medical tests and aggressive treatment. Hospice workers are experts at managing pain while maintaining the patient's awareness.

CONTINUING CARE RETIREMENT COMMUNITIES

Continuing care retirement communities (CCRCs), also sometimes called *life communities,* offer a variety of different kinds of care in one facility. CCRCs provide senior living, assisted living, and nursing home care. Residents are simply moved to the next level of care when needed. Often these different levels are housed in different buildings. These facilities can be a good choice for seniors who want to make plans now for how they will be cared for should they become ill. Entering a continuing care retirement community gives you the comfort of knowing exactly where you will be and knowing that your family and friends will not have to make decisions for you.

How It Works

Usually, a continuing care retirement community requires its residents to sign long-term contracts. The contract provides that the facility will care for the resident through any stage of care that is necessary. There is usually a large entrance fee ($40,000 and up) with monthly payments that can reach large amounts. Residents can buy their spot or rent it, meaning you can purchase it outright with a lump sum or you can pay an amount each month you stay there, like rent. The younger you are, the more cost effective it is to buy in.

The contracts can vary greatly. Some communities offer unlimited care of any kind needed for the resident's life. Others include a certain amount of nursing home care with anything needed beyond that period covered by additional fees. Some do not include any nursing home care at all and bill it all separately.

There are three types of CCRCs:

Type 1: Extensive Plan—This type of facility provides complete coverage for all your needs for the rest of your life. This is the most expensive plan available.

Type 2: Modified Plan—This type of CCRC offers the same services as Type 1, but not the same amount of service over your life. This type will place a limit on the type of nursing home care covered by your contract. Once you exceed it, you must pay for it (or your insurance must).

Type 3: Fee for Service Plan—This facility has the same services available, but you must pay for what you use.

Considering this Option

Continuing care communities are attractive because the continuing care they provide relieves you of any further decision-making and creates a long-term plan for care. There will be no last minute crisis in trying to find a good nursing home with an open bed. The downside is that these communities are very expensive and out-of-reach for most people. Once you are in a continuing care community and living in assisted-living or nursing home sections, you can *spend down* to Medicaid and have your care paid for that way. Medicare will cover some expenses, as will long-term care insurance. (See Chapter 2 for information about this.)

Problems

It is important to read the contract for continuing care very closely and make sure there are no hidden fees. You also need to consider what will happen to you if the continuing care community goes out of business. You must pay a substantial amount of money to enter the community. You do so assuming it will always be there to care for you. If the facility goes bankrupt, you will be out on the street and will have lost that investment. Talk to the continuing care community contact person about these concerns. Ask for information showing the corporation's financial well-being and stability. Speak to your local *ombudsman* (a state employee who works for nursing home and assisted living rights) about these concerns. (See Appendix D for a list.)

Evaluating

Continuing care communities are accredited by the *Continuing Care Accreditation Commission*. Contact them at **www.ccaconline.org**. If the nursing home or assisted-living facility sections accept Medicaid, they must be licensed and *accredited* by the state. Facilities that do not accept Medicaid are not subject to any state monitoring.

To evaluate a CCRC, follow these steps.

- Tour the entire facility, including the nursing home.
- Get a complete understanding of all fees and monthly payments.
- Find out what the policy is for transferring residents between levels of care.
- Carefully read and evaluate the contract.

- Get a complete listing of services that are included in your package.
- Find out if things like linens, transportation, and telephones are included.
- Ask for the fee increase history.
- Have a lawyer or accountant carefully read the annual report and balance sheet of the corporation.
- Ask if an actuarial study has been done, and if so, ask for a copy.
- Find out if the facility has been accredited by AAHSA (American Association of Homes and Services for the Aging).

–6–

SAFETY

One of your absolute, nonnegotiable rights is your right to be safe and well-cared for, no matter what your age or condition. Safety is a primary consideration for everyone, however, there are some issues that are particular to seniors.

SENIOR ABUSE

Abuse is mistreatment of a person either physically, emotionally, sexually, or mentally. Physical and sexual abuse are prohibited by law and include outright acts, such as hitting or punching, as well as neglect, such as failure to change sheets or to provide needed medical care. Abuse of seniors is a growing problem. Unfortunately, some senior abuse is perpetrated by family members who are providing home care for seniors.

> **SENIOR TIP**
>
> For more information, contact:
>
> **The National Center on Elder Abuse**
> 1201 15th Street NW Suite 350
> Washington, DC 20005-2800
> 202-898-2486
> **www.elderabusecenter.org**

If you or someone you know is being abused, contact your state *adult protective services*, a division of your department of family services or department of social services. A caseworker will be assigned within twenty-four hours of the initial call and will investigate the situation. If you or someone you care about is abused while in a nursing home, contact your local ombudsman.

Every senior has the right to be treated humanely and to live in safety. If you are ever in danger or are being harmed or neglected, the most important thing you can do is tell someone. Even if you are unable to pick up the phone and call for help, you must tell family, friends, or staff members at your facility about the problem and refuse to be quiet until someone listens to your concerns.

PROBLEMS IN A NURSING HOME

The problems that occur in nursing homes have been well-publicized as of late. Unfortunately, our nursing home system does not always provide the kind of quality care we want it to have. The nursing home resident is in a position where it is difficult to stand up for his or her rights.

When you enter a nursing home, you give up none of your civil rights. Under federal law, you have the right to:

- written information about your rights from the nursing home, including information about how to file a complaint; how to contact your state ombudsman; and, how to contact your state regulatory agency;
- written information about the services being provided as well as the daily basic rate;
- advance notice of any change in roommate or room assignment;
- an explanation of your right to create a health-care directive;
- information about your eligibility for Medicare and Medicaid;
- the results of the latest survey (inspection) of the nursing home;
- choose a personal physician;
- be informed about changes in your care or treatment;

- participate in planning or changes in your care or treatment;
- complain without fear of retribution;
- participate in resident and family groups;
- participate in social, religious, and community activities;
- privacy; and,
- visits from ombudsmen and family members.

It is very important to have someone else who can stand up for you, such as a family member or friend. There are ways to solve problems and care deficits in nursing homes, and the most effective way is to have someone else be your voice.

The first approach must be to speak with the *charge nurse* on duty and with any aides involved. Going directly to the person who has created the problem or who can best resolve it is always the best course of action. Do not let loose the cannons and go over the caregivers' heads without a good reason. Politely and calmly let them know what the problem is and make sure they fix it. Many problems are the result of mistakes or oversights and are not intentional.

If you feel a problem is severe; a problem continues to happen despite your complaints; or, if you feel there is simply an overwhelming number of problems you (or whoever is speaking for you) should speak to the director of nursing, the administrator, or to the staff social worker. Nursing homes must have a formal complaint and grievance process. Check with your state ombudsman about complaints and grievances if you do not get anywhere on your own.

Family Help

Nursing homes that accept Medicare must allow family members to form a *family council*—a group of residents' family members who meet to discuss problems, events, and solutions. The family council must be permitted to meet without staff present. Have your family member or friend go to the family council with your problem. If there is no family council, your family can start one. Residents also have the right to form *resident councils*. (These types of councils are required if the facility accepts Medicare.)

SENIOR TIP

Locate information about your local licensing agency at:
www.medicare.gov/nhcompare/home.asp

SENIOR TIP

Contact your local agency on aging for information about a nursing home advocacy group near you or check online at:
www.nccnhr.org.
For more information on the Centers for Medicare and Medicaid Services, visit:
www.hcfama.org

Government Help

If none of these approaches solves your problem, you need to go outside the nursing home for help. Contact your local ombudsman about your problem or concern. He or she will investigate your complaint and help you find ways to solve it. You may file a complaint with the state licensing agency and request that they perform an inspection. If any problems are found, the facility must fix them or face license suspension. If you are in immediate danger, the inspection must happen within forty-eight hours. If a resident has been harmed, the state has ten days to get the inspection done.

If you still do not feel your problem has been solved or if you have not been taken seriously, you can file a complaint with the federal *Centers for Medicare and Medicaid Services*, which oversees Medicare and Medicaid. This option is only available if the facility accepts Medicare or Medicaid. If you want to file a complaint about Medicaid fraud, contact your state's Medicaid fraud control unit. (Ask your local agency on aging for contact information.)

You may also wish to speak to a local nursing home advocacy group. These organizations support and help residents and their families.

When you file a complaint, you should:

- use dates and exact incidents whenever possible;
- include your contact information;
- indicate the length of an ongoing problem;
- include names of staff members if necessary;
- include the complete name and address of the facility;
- indicate the resident's name if you are a friend or family member writing on another person's behalf;
- specify if the problem is an emergency and if there is immediate danger;
- keep copies of all correspondence that you send; and,
- follow up by phone if you feel a response has not been given in an adequate amount of time.

Legal Help

As a last resort, you can always hire an attorney. You may be eligible for free legal services. (See Appendix C for referral services.) You may find that your attorney can get action just by sending a simple letter when you have been sending letters and making calls for weeks. A private attorney can also sue a nursing home for damages related to physical or emotional harm that you have suffered.

SCAMS

There are many scams that target seniors. Many of these are done over the phone or by people who come door-to-door. Some of these criminals have been known to steal or con seniors out of all their

SENIOR TIP

Consider adding your name to the federal *Do Not Call* telemarketing list at **www.DoNotCall.gov**. This list prevents telemarketers from calling your home.

funds or assets. Seniors are seen as targets because many of them live alone, welcome contact with people since they may feel lonely or isolated, or may be too trusting.

To protect yourself from scams and con artists, follow these rules.

- Never give out your credit card number, bank account number, or Social Security number to anyone unless you are making a purchase.
- Do not buy or agree to things over the phone. If it sounds like something you might be interested in, ask that they mail you something about it so you can review it on your own time and have someone else look at it if you have questions.
- Do not let people you do not know into your home. If the person at the door claims to be from a utility service and you did not call for service, ask to see identification. If he or

SENIOR TIP

Check out legitimacy of charities by contacting one of the following agencies:

Philanthropic Advisory Service
Council of Better
Business Bureaus
4200 Wilson Boulevard, Suite 800
Arlington, VA 22203-1838
703-276-0100
www.bbb.org

National Charities
Information Bureau
19 Union Square West, 6th Floor
New York, NY 10003-3395
212-929-6300
www.give.org

American Institute of
Philanthropy
4905 Del Ray Avenue, Suite 300
Bethesda, MD 20814
301-913-5200

she is not driving a company vehicle or is unable to provide a company ID, call the company and check while you ask the person to wait outside. (This is not being rude, it is being cautious.)

- Do not give away money or assets to people you do not know, even if you feel sorry for them. If you want to help other people, donate to known charities.
- Always rip up or shred any papers that have your credit card number, bank account number, or Social Security number on them before throwing them out.
- If you do not feel completely comfortable managing your own finances and financial decisions, ask a friend or family member for assistance.

NOTE: *Remember that if someone threatens you with physical harm, worry about protecting yourself first. Money and possessions can be replaced.*

CREDIT

Whenever you apply for credit, under the federal *Truth in Lending Act*, you must be told the finance charge and the annual percentage rate. If your lender fails to disclose this, you may be able to sue them for up to $1000. You may cancel any agreement for credit within three days if the contract requires you to put your home up as collateral or if a lien on your home could result from the contract (such as in a home repair or improvement deal).

To protect your rights:

- read the contract before signing;
- have someone else read it if you do not understand it;
- make sure all promises are in writing in the contract;

- keep copies of all contracts and correspondence; and,
- make sure you do not sign anything that has blank spaces (that can be filled in later).

NOTE: *It is illegal for a credit card company to send you a card you did not apply for.*

Stolen Credit Cards

The most you are liable for on a stolen credit card is $50, as long as you report it as soon as possible. Be sure to keep a list of your credit card companies and accounts in a safe place.

SENIOR TIP

For more information about protection from fraud, contact the Consumer Protection Bureau at **www.ftc.gov/bcp/bcp.htm**

Telemarketers

Telemarketers may only call between the hours of 8 am and 9 pm. It is best to just have a rule that you will not purchase anything offered by a telemarketer. Telemarketers cannot withdraw information from your bank account without your express verifiable permission. They cannot misrepresent what they are selling. Report telemarketer fraud to:

NFIC National Fraud Information Center
800-876-7060
www.fraud.org/welcome.htm

Home Repairs

Get referrals and shop around when seeking someone to do home repairs. Check references. Get all home repair contracts in writing. If the company seeks a deed of trust on your home (allowing them to place a lien if you do not pay), realize that you have three days to change your mind and cancel the contract.

PREDATORY MORTGAGE LENDERS

Predatory mortgage lenders are a specific group of scam artists that approach seniors who are in financial trouble—for example, who cannot pay their property taxes, are overwhelmed with medical bills, or cannot pay for urgent home repairs. These lenders know that these seniors need money and need it fast, and offer them loans that are secured with the senior's home. The loans often include very high fees, repayment terms that are impossible to meet, and outrageously high interest rates.

In general, if something sounds too good to be true, it is. Anyone who says bad credit is not a problem is someone to stay away from. Do not deal with lenders who contact you by phone. Avoid anything with a *balloon payment*—where you pay little upfront, but have to pay a large payment at a certain date in the future.

Always shop around for the best loan you can find and be sure to contact well-known local banks so you can determine the standard rate and terms. Read everything or have someone you trust read it for you. Even though you might be in financial trouble and need funds quickly, you can do yourself more harm by taking on a bad loan than by waiting to work with someone reputable.

If you do make a mistake and sign papers for a loan that you have second thoughts about, the federal *Truth in Lending Act* allows you to change your mind within three business days of the date you signed. You must do so in writing and send it to the lender. If you believe you have been the target of a lending scam, contact your state attorney general's office. (see Appendix D.)

HOME SAFETY

If you plan to live at home for as long as possible, you should take a careful look at the home. Things that are merely inconvenient now can be become dangerous as you age or if your health should change. There are modifications that can be done to make your home safe. Some home modifications are covered by Medicaid or Medicare, if you have a condition that necessitates the changes.

The following sets of lists identify—by area of your home—where home modifications should be considered.

Bathrooms

- handrails/grab bars by the toilet and tub;
- a seat in the tub or shower;
- transfer seat to allow easy access to the tub or shower;
- handheld shower head;
- nonslip rugs and decals on the floor and tub;
- overhead heat lamp;
- handles instead of knobs on faucets and drawers;
- nightlight;
- raised toilet seat;
- remove lock on door; and,
- dispenser for liquid soap and shampoo.

Kitchen

- rearrangement of items in kitchen cupboards so everything is within reach without bending or reaching (may require the addition of a free-standing cabinet);
- addition of bins that slide out from lower cabinets;
- plastic plates and glasses to minimize breakage;
- large letters and numbers for knobs on the stove;
- handles instead of knobs on faucets and drawers;
- placement of a fire extinguisher within reach of the stove;
- nightlight;
- potholders in easy reach of the stove and oven; and,
- elevated dishwasher (instead of having it built in on the floor, build it in a foot or two higher for easier access).

Laundry Room

- first floor location;
- top-loading dryer;
- laundry chute;
- smaller laundry baskets with grips on handles; and,
- laundry cart on wheels.

Bedroom

- located on the first floor;
- nightlight;
- telephone next to the bed;
- lamp next to bed;
- a chair or bench to make dressing easier;
- a hanging shoe rack;
- remove lock on door; and,
- hang as many things on hangers as possible instead of placing them in drawers.

All areas of the home

- higher watt bulbs in lamps and light fixtures;
- place electric cords out of the way and secure them against walls;
- windows that can easily be opened;
- ceiling fans instead of box fans;
- electric appliances that automatically shut off (such as an iron);
- remove furniture that is low to the ground and difficult to get out of;
- move tables with sharp edges away from high traffic areas or remove from the home;
- brightly-lit entrances to the home with handrails;
- lock or remove any casters or rollers on chairs or furniture;

- wall switches for lamps and overhead lighting;
- carbon monoxide detector;
- reflective tape on stairs;
- a plowing or shoveling service;
- a yard and garden service;
- smoke detectors;
- removal of area rugs that can cause tripping or catch on a walker;
- ramps in place of short groups of stairs;
- nightlights in hallways;
- handles/levers instead of door knobs;
- temperature controls on hot water heaters to prevent scalding;
- digital clocks with large displays;
- telephones with large number pads;
- bulletin board or wipe-off marker board for important phone numbers or medication schedule;
- handrails in hallways and near steps;
- large read out thermostat/air conditioning controller;
- large keypad remote control;
- a medical alarm system;
- doorways wide enough to accommodate a walker or wheelchair;
- reflective decals on sliding glass doors and on stair risers;
- an extendable gripping tool, to enable access to items on high shelves or items that fall to the floor;
- nonslip backing on area rugs;
- cordless phone;
- hearing aid compatible telephones;
- wall calendar with large numbers;
- magnifying glass with battery-powered light;

- remove all needed items from basement or attic storage;
- stopper for car in garage; and,
- reflectors at edge of driveway.

Because seniors are sometimes seen as easy targets for burglaries, it is important to make sure that your home has good locks, that all windows close tightly, and that you know how to get help quickly, either by calling 911 or using a home emergency remote system. It is also a good idea to be friendly with your neighbors so that if something is wrong, they will notice. If you plan on traveling, use timers for your lights; make sure your mail and paper are stopped or picked up; and, have someone check on your home regularly.

Heat

If you live in a colder climate, heat in the winter is essential. Gas and oil companies provide many programs that can be of assistance to seniors. Some of the more common programs include the following.

- *Third Party Notification*—the company will notify someone that you choose (such as a family member or friend) if you fail to pay your bill on time.
- *Hospitalization Assistance*—if you know you are going to be in the hospital or if you are unexpectedly in the hospital, you can notify the company and they will delay your billing for a period of time.
- *Senior Assistance*—this type of program offers debt forgiveness, emergency repairs or service, and more.
- *Payment Coordination*—bills can be adjusted so that they arrive at the same time as Social Security payments.
- *Budget Plans*—a budget plan averages your bills out over a year so that you are not hit with huge bills in the winter.

Service cannot be disconnected if doing so would pose a danger to your health. This rule normally applies only during winter months, November through March, or when the temperature falls below a certain point. State *public utility commissions* regulate your local utilities and are also sometimes called *public service commissions*. These commissions have written regulations that govern the utilities operating in your state.

While the regulations vary from state to state, they usually require written notice to a customer before terminating service, with an appeal process through the utility itself as well as the state commission. Disconnection is usually not permitted when the amount of a bill is in dispute or when the amount overdue is small.

SENIOR TIP

For information about assistance with heat bills for those with low incomes, contact *Low Income Home Energy Assistance Program* (LIHEAP) Clearinghouse National Energy Assistance Referral (NEAR) at 866-674-6327 or **www.acf.dhhs.gov/programs/liheap**

—7—

FAMILY ISSUES

Your family is probably one of the most important parts of your life, but sometimes conflicts can arise with family members. Understanding your rights and your options can help you cope with the situation and choose workable solutions.

GRANDPARENTS' VISITATION RIGHTS

Your grandchildren are even more special than you imagined they would be. The bond between a grandparent and grandchild is truly unique. But sometimes family conflicts can keep grandparents and grandchildren apart. This might happen because of a disagreement with the child's parent, because his or her parents divorce (often the grandparents on the noncustodial parent's side are left with little or no time with the children), or if one of the child's parents are deceased.

The first thing to do when confronting a barrier to your relationship with your grandchild is have patience. Yes, the situation is unfair, and yes, you are being denied the right to have a part in your grandchild's life, but usually these situations can and do resolve themselves over time. Give everyone some space and try to think about what you can do to repair the relationship or extend an olive branch.

Although your relationship with your grandchild's parents may not be able to be repaired, you may be able to convey that you will not bother them and just want to have time to nurture your grandchild. Sometimes some frank honesty might be called for. Ask point blank what the problem is. Try to have a discussion without anger. If none of this works, you might suggest seeing a counselor to help the family reach a solution and work out some of the underlying issues.

Many times parents object to grandparent visits because they believe the grandparent is trying to undermine their authority or somehow come between them and their children. If you can demonstrate that this is not your intent, you may be able to convince the parents to make you a part of your grandchild's life. Other family members can be useful in helping to broker a truce if you are unable to do so yourself.

If none of this works, you are unable to see or speak to your grandchild, and the problem is unresolved for some time, then you should think about speaking to an attorney about exercising your legal rights as a grandparent. The laws are different in every state regarding a grandparent's right to seek visitation. Some states permit any grandparent to ask the court for this right. Other states do not permit grandparents to ask for visitation if the child's parents are married and both oppose visitation.

Florida, Tennessee, North Dakota, and Washington have all had court cases deciding that state laws permitting grandparent visitation were unconstitutional. Some states only allow it if one of the child's parents has remarried and the child now is adopted by a stepparent.

If you are able to petition the court for visitation with your grandchild, you will need

SENIOR TIP

For more information and assistance with visitation rights, contact Grandparents' Rights Organization through:

www.grandparentsrights.org.

You can also contact:

Grandparents United for Children's Rights
137 Larkin St.
Madison, WI 53705
608-238-8751
www.geocities.com/Heartland/Prairie/6866

to prove to the court that it would be in the child's best interest to have visitation with you. The court will look at your relationship with the parents, your past, your own parenting, your lifestyle, and your existing bond with the child. Many of these cases settle without a trial, with the parties reaching some kind of compromise that allows contact. If you do go forward to a trial, it will be held in your state's family court. In most states you can represent yourself if you choose to, but it is not recommended.

If you are granted visitation by a court in one state, all other states must uphold that order, according to a 2000 U.S. Supreme Court case called *Troxel v. Granville.*

NOTE: *It is very important that you hire an attorney with experience handling grandparent visitation and custody cases in your state should you decide to file a petition.*

RAISING GRANDCHILDREN

More and more grandparents are raising their grandchildren. If you are raising your grandchild, it is important to have some legal safeguards in place.

Temporary Care

Some grandparents take on the care of a grandchild on a short-term basis—while the parent is away on a trip, for example. In this kind of situation, the most important thing you need is an authorization from the parent allowing you to seek medical care for the child. (See form 1 in Appendix G.) Without this document, you will be unable to obtain nonemergency care for the child (although emergency care will be accessible since pediatricians or emergency room providers will do what is necessary to save a child's life, save a limb, or prevent irreversible damage even without consent).

If you will be picking the child up from school, ask the parent to write a note authorizing you to do so. You should also obtain a copy of the child's health insurance card so that if you need to obtain medical care you will not have to worry about payment.

Permanent Care

If you are raising your grandchild and are taking over the role of a parent, there are several options available to you to legalize the relationship. It is important to take steps to legalize your relationship so that you obtain medical care for the child, handle his or her finances, and make important decisions about the child's life.

Guardianship

One option available to you is *guardianship*. You can petition the court to seek guardianship or the legal parent can give consent for you to take over guardianship. Guardianship is like custody, but it is not a completely permanent solution. When you are granted guardianship, you are given the authority to act as a parent, but the court will monitor and review your actions on an ongoing basis.

Custody

Another avenue is to obtain *custody* of your grandchild through your local family court. You can petition the court to seek custody or the legal parent can give consent. If you have the consent of the legal parent, the process is much smoother. It is more difficult for a grandparent to seek custody without consent because the courts always want to keep a child with his or her parents when possible.

SENIOR TIP

For support, assistance, and information about visitation, custody, or raising grandchildren, contact:

AARP Grandparent Information Center
601 E Street, NW
Washington, DC 20049
202-434-2296
www.aarp.org/confacts/programs/gic.html

Adoption

If you adopt your grandchild, you will need the consent of the legal parent or the state will need to terminate the parents' legal rights and place the child with you. You would then adopt him or her and he or she would become your legal child. Many grandparents are uncomfortable with the notion of adoption because it permanently severs the rights of the parents (although in some states, kinship agreements are honored that allow for ongoing contact between the child and other relatives, including birth parents).

Adoption can also be confusing for an older child who may have difficulty understanding how a grandparent has suddenly become his or her parent. Additionally, the adoption process is a long one and requires the involvement of social workers and home studies. There is no guarantee that once a child's relationship to the birth parents are terminated that you will be allowed to adopt, since the state is not obligated to place the child with you.

DIVORCE

Divorce is a difficult issue no matter what stage of your life you must confront it, but divorcing as a senior can be particularly difficult.

Deciding about Divorce

Choosing to get a divorce or accepting the fact that your spouse wants one is a huge hurdle. It is particularly huge if you have been married for a long period and are confronting tremendous change. Do not forget to consider counseling as a way to help you work through marital problems. You might think both of you are set in your ways, but it is definitely possible to teach an old dog new tricks.

If you do decide to go ahead with a divorce, consider *mediation*. Mediation is a process in which a neutral mediator helps you and your spouse come to an agreement about all of the issues involved in your divorce. Mediators are trained to help you look for solutions and compromises so that you can decide on your own all of the things a judge would have to decide in your case. Mediation is less expensive than a traditional divorce and can also be less stressful. To find a mediator, contact the *Association for Conflict Resolution* at **www.acrnet.org** or 202-464-9700.

Alimony

Once you are divorced, you are no longer entitled to receive payments from your spouse's Social Security or pension, unless the court orders that payments be made to you. (If you have been married over ten years, you will be entitled to Social Security payments.) If one of you has been the primary income earner in the marriage, the court can order alimony to help the other spouse survive financially. If your marriage has been a long one, and one spouse has not worked throughout the marriage, the court may order lifetime alimony, requiring the spouse who did work to financially support the other spouse for the rest of his or her life.

Property Division

Normally when a court considers how to divide property at the end of a marriage, *separate property* is first determined. Separate property is property that the spouses brought with them into the marriage. When dealing with a long-term marriage, little separate property remains, so most of the property will be divided between the spouses. Different states divide property in different ways. States like California use the *community property rule*, which gives half of everything to each spouse. Other states use a standard that divides things in a way that is *equitable* or fair.

Coping with Divorce

As you cope with a divorce, you will find that many things in your life must change. If your marriage was a long-term one, you must learn to live on your own again and do the household chores and tasks that your spouse always performed. This can be a dramatic adjustment. Seek out support from family and friends. Become active in your community, make new friends, and discover new interests. Learning to cope with the divorce can take quite a while, but is manageable if you have people to help you through it.

REMARRIAGE

Whether you have lost a spouse or have been divorced, choosing to remarry is a big step. It is one that has important implications not only for you, but for your children as well.

Prenuptial Agreements

A *prenuptial agreement* is really a must-have for many people who are remarrying. When you remarry as a senior, both you and your new spouse have assets and probably have plans to pass them on to your own children. You do not want to risk losing those assets in a divorce. Additionally, it is important to realize that many second marriages are not successful, so it makes sense to plan in advance for what will happen to your assets should you divorce.

Prenups can also be important to your children. They may question your desire to remarry and may feel that you (and consequently, they) are more protected if there is a prenup in place.

Wills

When remarrying, it is important to have a new will drafted. If you do not have a will, the court will divide your estate according to state laws, which gives a large portion to the spouse. If you and your spouse want to pass most of your assets to your children, it is important to have wills drawn up that give this direction. Understand that you cannot disinherit your spouse if he or she wants to collect from your estate.

There is a spousal *right of election* that gives a spouse the right to take a percentage of the estate, even if he or she is specifically given nothing in a will. However, this is only an option, and if you and your spouse agree you will not use this option and it is not elected, your estate will pass to your children as you direct in your will. There is no way to prevent your spouse from using this option, so if you are concerned you may wish to discuss lifetime gifts and transfers with your attorney.

Health-Care Directives

Chapter 8 discusses the importance of health-care directives, which give others the power to make medical decisions for you if you are ever unable to make them yourself. Most people want their spouses to make these decisions, but many older people choose their children. It is also possible to name your spouse and your children together and ask them to make decisions together. If you remarry, it is important to have a new health-care directive drawn up, naming your spouse or your children as the people who will make decisions for you.

COHABITATION

Many seniors decide to live with another person in a roommate situation to help share expenses or to avoid loneliness. Other seniors are in committed relationships and living together, but choose not to formally marry. If you and another person live together, you can take some steps to protect yourselves and set parameters for your relationship.

Roommate Agreements

If you live together, you may decide to complete *a roommate agreement*. This is a document that lays out all the financial responsibilities for each person, so that it is completely clear how you will pay bills, share expenses, and share household responsibilities.

Your roommate agreement should be tailored to your particular situation and should include agreements that you make. The agreement can be helpful if a conflict comes up or if your relationship ends, since it will provide a clear roadmap for how financial issues are to be solved.

Roommate agreements are also helpful in a personal way. You may each come to the relationship used to living in your own particular ways. If you use a personalized roommate agreement, you can create a plan that will help you each understand your day-to-day responsibilities. Your agreement can specify who is supposed to take out the trash, who will do the cooking, or even address small points of contention like where the car keys will be kept. It is important to note that these smaller issues of daily life are not things a court would be likely to enforce, but it can be helpful simply to write them down on a piece of paper so you are both clear about how you will organize your lives.

Powers of Attorney

Depending on what your relationship is like, you may wish to execute powers of attorney that will allow both of you to handle financial and legal affairs for each other. For example, if you move into your partner's condo and he or she is hospitalized, you would want to have the ability to make the yearly payment on his or her behalf or pay for an assessment. If you do not have power of attorney, you cannot access your partner's bank account to pay any bills on his or her behalf. You also cannot cash any checks that come for him or her. (See Chapter 8 for more information about powers of attorney.)

STEPFAMILY

Stepfamilies are a common part of many people's lives, but that does not mean that it is always easy to understand how to negotiate and deal with the relationships that stepfamilies create.

Your Remarriage

If you have remarried and your spouse has children or grandchildren, they are suddenly part of your family. Stepfamily relations can be tricky when you have to deal with issues involving your spouse's former spouse. You do not want to take anyone's place, but you do want to create your own place in the family.

It is often best to take things in small steps and try to have a lot of patience as you work through stepfamily issues. Although you are linked to this new family by marriage, you have no legal ties to them. So your spouse's children will not inherit from you unless you specifically designate this in your will. You have no legal right to visitation with your stepgrandchildren—only your spouse has this right. The same is true vice versa with your children and grandchildren and your spouse.

SENIOR TIP

For support and information about stepfamilies, contact:

Stepfamily Association of America
650 J Street, Suite 205
Lincoln, NE 68508
800-735-0329
www.saafamilies.org

Your Children's Remarriage

Another way stepfamilies can enter into your life is when your children remarry and the new spouse has children. These are your stepgrandchildren. Different families handle this relationship in different ways. In some families, the stepgrandchildren are treated exactly like the grandchildren, while in other families, a distinction is made, particularly if the stepgrandchildren have their own grandparents. You have no legal relationship to your stepgrandchildren and have no right to visitation with them, but it can be difficult to treat children in the same family differently. The best plan is to talk candidly with your child and his or her new spouse about how you will handle things.

—8—

PLANNING FOR THE FUTURE

Having a will made, preparing powers of attorney, and having a health-care directive prepared are important steps everyone needs to take to plan for the future. It is your right to decide who will make health and legal decisions for you should you become unable to make them for yourself.

MAKING DECISIONS

Deciding who you want to pass your property to when you die and choosing someone to make medical decisions for you if you are ever unable are decisions that require a lot of thought. You may find that these are issues you want to discuss with your friends or family members, or you may feel they are private matters. Whatever you decide, it is important to talk to an attorney about these matters. Not only can an attorney create the documents in the format required by your state, but he or she can advise you about matters such as estate taxes.

When you see an attorney about these matters, it is important to remember that you are the client. Many people bring a spouse, son, daughter, or other family member along with them to the meeting, and while having support can be helpful, you must remember that the decisions you will make are yours alone. Some seniors let their family member do all the talking. While this is ok if what is being conveyed are your wishes, sometimes the person with you can try to impose his or her own choices and feelings onto you. Make sure that the attorney hears what you really want.

WILLS AND ESTATES

A *will* is a legal document that disposes of a person's belongings after death. A will allows you to express your wishes about how you would like to divide your belongings among your family, friends, and favorite charities.

Writing a will is a part of what is called *estate planning*. Estate planning involves the arrangement and disposal of all your assets with the idea of maximizing what you pass by minimizing cost and reducing or avoiding taxes. An attorney can assist you in dealing with your assets to minimize capital gains taxes. An attorney can also set up trusts, arrange for charitable gifts, and help you understand the probate process (the process through which the court approves a will and allows property to be divided).

Most states require that for a will to be valid:

- you must be of sound mind when you sign it;
- that it be witnessed by two people; and,
- that it be in writing and actually signed by you.

An attorney can explain to you what would happen to your belongings if you died without a will (known as dying *intestate*). This differs from state to state, but in general, they would be divided between your spouse and children, with the amounts determined by your state laws.

It is also often a good idea to create a letter with instructions about how small items of personal property should be divided. A will usually does not get into detail about who will get the books, dishes, and towels—things that are not of great value, but may have particular meaning or may be needed by one family member more than another. Pets are another item that should be included, with instructions as to whom will become the pet's new owner.

In the will, you will choose an *executor,* who is a person who will work to carry out your wishes by distributing your property as you have directed. This person will work closely with the attorney handling the estate, and will invest a lot of time and effort into handling your affairs for you. It is usually a good idea to select someone who is younger than you are. You may also choose an alternate in case the person you name cannot take on the responsibility, is deceased, or does not wish to handle it.

If you have a spouse, it is a good idea that he or she has a will drawn up as well. You each need to have your own wills. It is a good idea to have the same attorney create both, so the two wills coordinate and handle things in a similar manner.

In your will you can leave your possessions and assets to anyone you want. You are not required to leave things to your children or to include all of your children. Additionally, you are not required to leave things to your spouse, however, in most states if you are married (even if you are separated) spouses are given what is called a *right of election,* which means that if you do not leave your spouse a certain amount in your will, he or she has the right to take an *election amount* (an amount set by state law) even if the will does not provide for it.

NOTE: *Wills have no effect on life insurance. To change the beneficiary of a life insurance policy, you must obtain a charge of beneficiary form from your insurance company.*

Some people include instructions in a will about burial or cremation preferences. While it is a good idea to write down your wishes, a will is not the best place for this information. Unless you distribute copies of your will to your family, they will not know your wishes at the time of your death when those choices are being made. The best plan is to discuss your choices with your family, or at the very least, to leave a note that will be found before any decision is made. These options may not guarantee that your wishes will be followed. Even if you include them in your will, it will not be legally binding. To change your will you must: either write a new one (it is usually wise to destroy the old one) or execute a codicil or amendment to an existing will, which adds your changes or additions.

Living Trust

A *living trust* is one type of estate planning in which you place some or all of your property in trust. You choose a trustee who will manage the property. In some cases, you can be the trustee. You can continue to use the property in the trust. Once you die, the property passes to the beneficiary you name, does not go through probate, and is not subject to estate tax (which is being phased out). Most living trusts are revocable, which means you can change your mind about them. Talk to your attorney about whether a living trust might make sense for you.

SENIOR TIP

Get more information about living trusts at:

www.ftc.gov/bcp/conline/pubs/services/livtrust.htm

or

www.oag.state.ny.us/seniors/living_trust.html

Estate Tax

The *estate tax* is a tax charged on taxable assets that are passed at your death. Congress passed legislation that has *rolled back* (repealed) the tax through 2010, but if further legislation is not passed, it will come back into effect.

SENIOR TIP

Calculate how the estate tax will impact you using an online calculator:

www.banksite.com/calc/estate

(In 2004, only estates over $1.5 million had to pay the tax.)

Generation-Skipping Tax

In addition to the estate tax, there is another tax that is not well understood by most people, called the *generation-skipping tax* (GST). This tax is applied when a bequest is made to someone who is more than one generation away. For example, if you leave something to a grandchild, the gift is considered to have *skipped* a generation. This is important because normally people leave things to their children, estate tax is collected and then when their children die, they leave it to their children (your grandchildren) and another round of estate tax is collected.

The generation-skipping tax seeks to make up for the round of estate tax the government would be missing out on if you leave assets to grandchildren by applying a flat 55% tax on the amount of gifts over the current estate tax exemption. Just as with the estate tax, this tax will be phased out in 2010, but will reappear in 2011 unless legislation is passed.

Gift Tax

It is important to understand that Congress has not repealed the gift tax law, which applies to gifts you make during your life. Under current legislation, you can give up to $11,000 to different individuals per year without having to pay tax, with a lifetime total for all recipients of $1 million. If married, both you and your spouse can give $11,000 allowing a total annual gift of $22,000 to one person with no direct tax consequence. If you would like to give large gifts during your lifetime, consult with an attorney about the best way to do so.

NOTE: *It is difficult to trace cash gifts, but gifts given via check or transfers of stock or property are easily traceable.*

TRUSTS

Trusts are a way to give money or property away while maintaining some control over the asset. Usually, a trust holds the asset or money and pays income to the *beneficiary* (person who benefits from the trust). A *testamentary trust* is one that is set up after a person's death, through instructions in a will.

Many people have heard of a *living trust*, which people may see as a way to avoid *probate* (the process through which a will is validated by a court). The owner of the property creates the trust and acts as trustee, controlling everything in the trust. If he or she dies or becomes unable to manage it, a secondary trustee steps in. The creator of the trust can terminate the trust at any point. The advantages of a living trust are that you can completely control the assets you place in it and end it at any point. A living trust also cannot be *contested* (challenged in court), which makes it appealing to people who wish to leave out key family members. The assets in the trust remain in the trust after the creator's death and do not pass through probate, but they are taxable. Many people favor these kinds of arrangements because there is no court involvement.

An *irrevocable trust* is a trust that cannot be changed once it is created. This can be a useful tool in estate planning. If you are considering a trust of any kind, you need to speak to an attorney who specializes in estate law.

POWERS OF ATTORNEY

A power of attorney is a legal document signed by you that gives authority to someone else to manage your financial, business, or personal affairs. A power of attorney becomes important if you become ill for an extended period. For example, if you are unexpectedly in the hospital for three weeks, you will not be able to pay your bills, deposit checks, or renew your car registration. A power of attorney gives authority to the person you name to handle these kinds of things for you.

There are two main types of powers of attorney: *springing* and *durable*. A springing power of attorney can be signed today but not take effect until some event occurs, such as you becoming incapacitated, or on a specific date. A durable power of attorney becomes valid once it is signed and continues indefinitely.

Many states have their own power of attorney form, so it is best to consult with an attorney who can create one for you that meets your state's requirements. (See Chapter 12 for information about how to locate an attorney.) Some states have what is called a *short form* power of attorney, which is a shortened version of the state's regular form, designed to be easier to understand and complete, and is often specifically designed for seniors.

The power of attorney will give the person you choose the right to manage your bank accounts, change your investments, pay your bills, and so on. A power of attorney does not deal with health-care decisions. (See next section on health-care directives.)

It is a good idea to execute a power of attorney and keep it on hand for when it is needed. Situations can arise unexpectedly and it is best to be prepared. It is important that you completely trust whoever you name in your power of attorney, because he or she will have access to your money and assets. Make sure that you talk this over with the person you are naming to make sure it is a responsibility he or she is willing to take on.

NOTE: *When you are granting power of attorney on a bank account, your bank will usually have the necessary forms and can help you complete it and will notarize it, making it effective immediately.*

HEALTH-CARE DIRECTIVES AND PROXIES

Some seniors believe that there is no reason to create health-care directives or proxies because if they become unable to make decisions, their family members will do so for them. In most states, family members are allowed to make decisions for a patient who is not cognizant. However, if family members disagree or do not know what the patient's desires are, the situation can become difficult, confusing, and legally complicated.

Other times seniors see no reason to create a health-care directive since they believe the medical staff will care for them appropriately. It is important to remember that doctors and hospitals focus on maintaining and preserving life. They try to manage pain, but they will not and cannot decide to stop medical care and allow a patient to die. For many people, the thought of being kept alive by machines when they have no hope of recovery or when they would not be conscious is horrendous. To prevent this, you a need health-care directive to ensure that you are cared for in ways that meet your own personal wishes. (These types of documents have different names and vary from state to state.)

Living Will

A *living will* is a document that describes a patient's wishes about life-saving or life-sustaining medical care when he or she is terminally ill or in a permanent vegetative state. The document can specify the types of treatments and procedures that the patient does not want to receive. It can also dictate the type of pain management a patient wishes to receive. In some states, a living will may be called a *declaration*.

> **SENIOR TIP**
>
> Partnership for Caring (**www.partnershipforcaring.org**, 800-989-9455) is an organization that provides varied information regarding state-specific wills.

Health-Care Proxy

A *health-care proxy* is similar to a power of attorney. It appoints a *proxy*, a person who will make health care decisions for the patient when he or she is unable to do so.

Advanced Directives

An *advanced directive* is usually a living will and health-care proxy combined into one document. Some states specifically recognize one document or another, but all states are bound to respect a person's wishes (based on the famous *Cruzan* Supreme Court case, where Nancy Cruzan's parents' sought the ability to turn off her life support).

> **SENIOR TIP**
>
> Once you have signed the appropriate form(s), it is important to give copies of them to your doctors and to provide copies to hospitals when you are admitted. You may also wish to register your living will with the *U.S. Living Will Registry* (**www.uslivingwillregistry.com**), a free service that places your advanced directive in a secure site so that medical workers can access it anywhere, anytime.

It is always best to have an attorney prepare these documents, since he or she will understand what type of document is best accepted in your state.

To revoke a directive, rip it up or sign a document that states you revoke all prior directives and give a copy of this to all the health-care providers to whom you have given copies of the previous directive.

DNR Orders

If you enter a hospital, you have the option of instructing the staff not to resuscitate you should you go into cardiac arrest or stop breathing. A *do not resuscitate* (DNR) order is entered into your chart. This is a decision that should not be made lightly. Discuss your health condition with your care providers and find out your prognosis. Some people want their lives to be extended whenever possible, while others feel strongly that they do not want this kind of intervention.

ORGAN DONATION

If you would like to donate your organs after you die or if you would like to donate your body to research, you need to complete an organ donation agreement. In many states you can simply complete and sign the back of your driver's license. In other states you are required to fill out a separate form. If you do not authorize this, your next of kin will be permitted to make this decision.

To donate your entire body for research purposes, contact a medical school in your area. They can explain the program and provide releases and forms for you to sign. Body donation has been in the news, so you may wish to get details about where and how your remains will be used. That way you are certain your remains will be used for medical research purposes and not sold for other purposes.

> **SENIOR TIP**
>
> Visit **www.organdonor.gov** for more information about organ donation.

If you do want to donate your organs or your body, it is important to discuss this with your family members so they know and understand your wishes in advance.

AUTOPSIES

Some people feel strongly that they do not wish to have an autopsy performed on their bodies after they die. Autopsies are actually rare and are usually only done when someone dies in a way that is not explained (so that there might a crime involved) or if medical science can benefit from understanding what exactly happened. The only time an autopsy is legally required is if a crime may have been involved. The family has the ability to say *no* to any other request that is made. If this is a subject you feel strongly about, discuss it with your family members and make sure they understand your wishes.

–9–

LOSS OF A SPOUSE

The loss of a spouse is one of the most traumatic times in a person's life. When your spouse dies, the last thing you want to think about are legal matters like wills and transferring ownership of cars to your name. This chapter is designed to help you understand what your rights are now so should you ever be in the sad position of losing a spouse, you will already know the basic information about how to handle certain problems.

FUNERAL LAW

Planning a funeral is challenging, because the people doing the planning are under great stress. When you are under a lot of stress it is hard to focus on what your rights are, but you actually do have a lot of rights when it comes to funerals. Learning about these rights in advance can help you speak up for yourself should you ever be in the position of having to plan a funeral.

Funeral homes are regulated by the federal *Funeral Rule*, which includes these requirements.

- The funeral home must provide a general price list in writing or over the phone.
- The funeral home must inform you that embalming *is not required* in most cases, but that if the body is not embalmed, it will require direct burial or cremation.

- The funeral home must inform you of fees for items they rent or purchase on your behalf and whether a service fee is included.
- A casket is not required for cremation. A container made of cardboard or canvas is all that is required, and funeral homes must make this option available.
- Customers must be allowed to choose only the services or goods they want.
- The funeral home must disclose state law requirements.
- An itemized statement must be provided showing the individual and total prices.
- A funeral home cannot tell you that a procedure will indefinitely preserve a body unless it actually will, and it may not tell you a casket will keep out dirt, water, and so on unless it really will.

Many people choose to preplan and prepay for their own funerals. This is an option you or your spouse may wish to consider. In doing so, you relieve your family of the burden and cost of making these decisions. Some people leave instructions for their funerals in their wills. Be aware that this kind of instruction is not binding and may not even be read until after the funeral. To be sure your wishes are carried out, you should discuss them with family members or preplan your funeral.

OBITUARIES

Many people are surprised to learn that obituaries are not free. If you want one to run, you must pay for it in the same way you would a classified ad. Someone in your family will need to call the obituary department of your local paper or the funeral director may handle it. You will need to have the following information available:

- the deceased's full name (and maiden name, if applicable);
- date of birth;
- date of death;
- place of death;
- cause of death if you wish to include it (some people prefer to simply indicate whether it was a long illness, short illness, or unexpected);
- name of spouse (and maiden name, if applicable);
- names of children and their spouses;
- names of grandchildren (if you wish to include them);
- date, place, and times of funeral home visitations;
- date, place, and time of burial, (if public);
- any important facts or achievements of the deceased; and,
- where donations should be sent if they are preferred over flowers.

Some people write their own obituaries and leave them for their family members to use.

SAFETY

After a spouse dies, personal safety may not be one of the things you think about, but obituaries are often used by criminals to target homes to rob. Make sure that someone can stay at your home while you are at your spouse's funeral, memorial service, or wake. Do not welcome people into your home if you do not know them, even if they say they would like to pay you a condolence call. If you are uncomfortable being home alone after a funeral, ask a family member or friend to stay with you for a few days.

APPLYING FOR BENEFITS

If you have lost a spouse, you are eligible to receive Social Security payments, as well as death benefits, through your spouse's employer. If your spouse has retirement accounts, (even if he or she is not being paid from them yet), you are also entitled to receive this money. Contact the plan administrator at your spouse's place of business for information about how to apply.

You can begin to receive Social Security payments as a widow or widower as early as age 60, or age 50 if you are disabled. When you apply, ask if you qualify for any of the following:

- lump-sum death benefit;
- life pension to widow/widower over age 60;
- payments to widows, widowers or divorcees over age 50 who are disabled; or,
- Medicare.

NOTE: *Social Security payments end upon death, so if your spouse continues to receive payments, you need to notify Social Security.*

SENIOR TIP

To apply for spousal Social Security benefits, use the online form at:

www.ssa.gov/retirement.html

You will also need to apply for life insurance benefits if your spouse had a life insurance policy. Call the insurance company and explain the situation. They will tell you what you need to provide. Usually the items include:

- death certificate;
- policy number; and,
- some proof of identity.

NOTE: *Not only will your spouse have the life insurance he or she took out and paid for, but he or she probably also has several smaller policies provided at no cost by his or her employer, credit card companies, banks, and other institutions. AAA provides an insurance policy with* *membership as well. If you are not sure what policies are in effect, call or have a friend or family member call banks and credit card companies to inquire.*

PROBATE

After a spouse dies, you will need to locate his or her will. There is no great hurry for this, but many people feel that they want to move along and get the affairs taken care of so they can begin to heal. If you do not know where the will is, ask your spouse's attorney. Your spouse's attorney may have the original will in his or her office or it may have been filed with your local probate court for safekeeping.

The original will *must* be located. A copy is not sufficient. If your spouse created a handwritten will, you will need to consult with your attorney to determine if it will be valid in your state. You will also need to make sure you have the most current will and any *codicils* (amendments and changes) that were made to it.

Once the will has been located, you will want to talk to an attorney who specializes in probate and estates. The attorney you hire will represent the *executor*, the person named in the will to distribute the belongings. If your spouse died with few assets, you may be able to handle it yourself, through a special small estates process. Check with your local probate court to find out what your state's rules are.

The will must be approved by the court and all the actions taken by the executor will be examined by the court. The court first makes sure that the will is authentic; that it was signed by your spouse of his or her free will; and, that it was witnessed properly. Then the court gives the executor the power to distribute your spouse's belongings. All relatives are formerly notified of the process. The executor decides whether to sell property or pass it on as it is. This choice becomes necessary if the will lists cash bequests to specific people, but the deceased owned items other than just cash.

Before the court will allow the executor to distribute the assets of the estate, the estate is *frozen*. This means that money cannot be taken out of bank accounts, safe deposit boxes cannot be opened, and investments and personal property cannot be removed from a home. This happens so that the court can be sure all the bills are paid before money is distributed. Allowances are usually paid to surviving spouses so that they can continue to meet their expenses.

Not all of your spouse's assets will go through probate. The types of items that do not pass through probate and are not subject to the will include:

- property that you own jointly with right of survivorship;
- property in trust;
- assets that have a named beneficiary;
- life insurance;
- 401(k)s;
- pensions; and,
- annuities.

Not all estates must go through formal probate. Most states have a dollar amount (such as $100,000) under which an estate does not need to go through probate. The probate process on average takes several months.

You have the right to hire your own attorney during the probate process to watch out for your rights. Remember, the attorney for the estate represents the executor. If you believe that the will is not valid, if you have been cut out of the will, or if you believe the executor is not handling things fairly, you should hire your own attorney to represent you throughout the process.

If your spouse dies without a will, the court appoints an *administrator* who distributes your spouse's property according the laws of the state (usually dividing it between spouse and children). If the estate is small, it can be handled through a special small estate administration process. It is also possible that you may not need to go to probate court at all. If all of your spouse's assets were also in your name, they may pass directly to you without any approval by the court.

CHANGING OWNERSHIP

It is possible to change ownership on some things without dealing with the probate process. For example, to change the name on the title of a car, most states require a copy of the death certificate and an affidavit from the surviving spouse. Contact your local department of motor vehicles for details and forms. Make sure you change your auto insurance to reflect this change as well.

Items that are owned as *joint tenants with right of survivorship* (such as homes and many investments) can be transferred to the surviving spouse's name with a death certificate. Because joint bank accounts will be frozen, you will be unable to change these accounts to your name alone until probate has completed.

Remember to change names on utility bills, on credit cards, and to change beneficiaries on your own life insurance policies.

–10–

DISCRIMINATION AND DISABILITIES

You have the right to be treated fairly regardless of your age or physical abilities. But discrimination does happen, so it is important to understand the protections available to you. Unfortunately, there are instances in which older people are treated differently simply because of their age. There are federal, state, and local laws designed to offer protection from age discrimination, and while there is some protection available through these laws, it is important to understand that all kinds of discrimination are not prohibited. For example, if someone is mean or unpleasant to an older person simply because of his or her age, this behavior might be morally wrong, but it is not legally wrong. You need to be aware of those incidents of discrimination that are legally wrong and learn what you can do should you be subjected to age discrimination.

EMPLOYMENT DISCRIMINATION

The *Age Discrimination in Employment Act* is a federal law that prohibits employers from making hiring, firing, compensation, or promotion decisions based on age. Employers also cannot use age to limit, segregate, or classify employees so that they would be deprived of employment opportunities or negatively affected in their employment status. (For example, it would be against the law to move workers of a certain age to a separate building.)

The law protects anyone age forty or older who works for an employer with twenty or more employees. The law does not prohibit an employer from asking a potential employee his or her age or date of birth. There are some exceptions to the law that have to do with mandatory retirement ages. Currently, mandatory retirement ages can be as low as age 55. The law allows employers to set mandatory retirement ages in two situations:

- for *bona fide* executives or high policy-making positions that carry a retirement benefit of at least $44,000 or
- positions in which age can affect job performance and public safety is involved in some way, such as with police officers or pilots. The employer must show that all or nearly all workers above the mandatory retirement age lack the qualifications for the job or that it would be very difficult for the employer to be able to test each person to determine if he or she still has the necessary job qualifications.

Another federal law, the *Older Workers Benefit Protection Act*, prohibits employers from denying benefits to workers because of age. Employers can reduce a worker's benefits because of his age only if the cost of the reduced benefits is equal to the cost of benefits currently provided to younger workers. Examples of discrimination include being given a lower salary than someone in an equivalent position with equivalent experience; being denied an interview or not hired because of age; or, being fired because of age.

> **SENIOR TIP**
>
> You can file a complaint at a local EEOC office. Find your local office by checking the government pages of your phone book or online at
>
> **www.eeoc.gov/offices.html**

If you believe that you have been discriminated against by an employer or potential employer because of age, contact an employment attorney and file a complaint with the *Equal Employment Opportunity Commission* (EEOC) within 180 days of the incident.

HOUSING DISCRIMINATION

The *Age Discrimination Act* prohibits discrimination on the basis of age against anyone participating in a federally funded housing program or activity. What this means is that if you are applying for or are living in HUD housing, you cannot be denied housing or evicted because of your age. However, the federal *Fair Housing Act* does not include age as a protected category, so there is no relief available to someone who is denied housing or evicted by a private landlord because of age.

Many states and municipalities have laws preventing housing discrimination based on age. Some of these locations include:

- California
- Connecticut
- Delaware
- District of Columbia
- Hawaii
- Massachusetts
- Milwaukee
- Montana
- New Hampshire
- New York
- North Dakota
- Palm Beach County, Florida
- Pennsylvania
- Vermont
- Virginia
- Wisconsin

Check with your municipal government to find out if you have any protections through local law. The types of discrimination covered vary by state and municipality, but can include things like the right not to be denied housing due to age, the right not to be evicted solely because of age, and the requirement that you must be treated the same as other tenants with regard to rent and other rules. To prove housing discrimination, you need to be able to show that you were treated differently than someone else who was similar to you in most ways, except he or she was younger. For example, if you applied for an apartment and you were denied, but it was rented to someone who had the same income as you and the same quality of references, you might have a claim.

To report a housing discrimination claim, contact your state attorney general's office or your state housing department.

CREDIT DISCRIMINATION

The *Equal Credit Opportunity Law* is a federal law that makes it illegal to discriminate against a person in lending or credit because of his or her age. Creditors are permitted to ask your age and date of birth, but that information cannot be used when deciding whether to give you credit. This means that lenders and creditors must apply the same standards to all applicants. The law applies to banks, lenders, credit unions, car dealers, department stores, credit card companies, appliance dealers, finance companies, and anyone else who regularly grants credit. For example, a bank could not refuse to give you a mortgage because of your age, or a credit card company could not charge you a higher interest rate because of your age.

If you believe you have been denied credit or treated in a discriminatory way by a lender or creditor, contact your state attorney general's office or hire an attorney.

DISABILITIES

Living with a disability impacts every area of your life—your income, your social life, your health care, and where you live. Understanding your rights and the types of assistance available to you can make living with a disability more manageable.

Discrimination

There are many federal laws in place that provide protections for people with disabilities. One of the most important is the *Americans with Disabilities Act*. The law defines *disabled* as a physical or mental impairment that substantially limits one or more major life activities and includes difficulties with vision, hearing, speech, breathing, performing life activities, walking, caring for oneself, or working. The law also covers people who have had some kind of impairment in the past, such as someone who is a cancer survivor, as well as people who are viewed as having an impairment, such as someone with a facial disfigurement. This law prohibits discrimination in the workplace against people who are disabled and requires employers to make *reasonable accommodations* to allow disabled people to work for them. Complaints under this part of the law must be filed with the *Equal Employment Opportunity Commission* within 180 days. (see Appendix A.)

The law also requires that state and local governments make all of their programs and services equally available to the disabled. This means that public buildings must be made accessible for disabled people and that government programs must be accessible to people with vision, hearing, or speech problems. Public transportation must be accessible to people with disabilities. The law also applies to public businesses such as hotels, restaurants, stores, movie theaters, private schools, and doctors' offices and says that these businesses must not discriminate against the disabled and that new or modified buildings should be accessible. Violations of these provisions of the law must be filed with the Department of Justice within 180 days.

The federal *Fair Housing Act* prohibits housing discrimination against the disabled and covers renting, selling, and buying homes and dwellings as well as financing for home purchases. The law requires landlords to permit disabled people to have animal companions that assist them even if pets are prohibited. The law also allows tenants to make modifications to rental property (including common areas, such as halls or lobbies) that relate to their disability, such as installing handrails and widening doorways. Complaints about violations of this law must be made to the *Office of Fair Housing*. (see Appendix A.)

ACCESS FOR THE DISABLED

Government-funded agencies must make their programs and offices accessible to the disabled and public businesses must try to accommodate the disabled, but what does this really mean in the life of a disabled person? The fact is, although a lot of protections are in place, most buildings are not designed with the disabled in mind (although modern buildings are far more accessible than older buildings). Publicly funded agencies and programs must make arrangements to accommodate a disability. If you find that you cannot access a certain building or location, call (or have a family member call) and explain your situation and ask what accommodations they can make.

Accessing Wheelchairs and Assistance

Most medical buildings provide wheelchairs for those visiting the facility. If you need assistance getting from the entrance to the office, a call in advance can usually arrange for someone to be present and assist you. Some public spaces, like airports and shopping malls, also have wheelchairs available for use.

Recognize that most stores, restaurants, and other places are happy to provide you with any extra assistance that you need. Department stores, for example, often have personal shoppers who can collect clothes for you to try on while you wait in a dressing room. Ushers at movie theaters can assist you to a seat. Servers at restaurants can make sure food is prepared to your specifications if you have a disability that impacts your ability to chew or restricts your diet.

Disabled Parking

If you are blind or have an ambulatory disability (one that makes it difficult for you to walk), you are entitled to apply for a handicap parking hang tag or license plate. In most states you need to complete an application form and have a medical form completed by your physician. The license plate permit is the easiest to use since you do not need to think about hanging up your tag when you park. A hang tag is useful as well, since you can take it with you if you are riding in another person's car.

Handicap parking spaces are reserved for people with handicap license plates or hang tags. It is a misdemeanor in most states to park in one of these spaces without a hang tag or license. Handicap parking spaces must be clearly marked with printing on the ground as well as with a signpost.

SENIOR TIP

If you have questions or complaints about disability access, contact:

The Access Board
1331 F Street, NW, Suite 1000
Washington, DC 20004-1111
202-272-0080
http://www.access-board.gov

In some cities, vehicles with handicap plates or hang tags are not required to pay when parking at street meters. In some cities, payment is required, but the vehicle is permitted to remain for a certain period of time past the metered time at no charge. Check with local parking authorities to learn the details in your area.

Voting

The *Voting Accessibility for the Elderly and Handicapped Act* requires that polling places be accessible to people with physical disabilities. If the polling place is not accessible, arrangements must be made so that the voter can cast a ballot.

DISABILITY BENEFITS

The Social Security Program provides two types of benefits for the disabled. *Social Security Disability* (SSD) pays benefits to people who have become disabled and can no longer do the kind of work they were doing before. *Supplemental Security Income* (SSI) provides basic income to people who are elderly or disabled, without regard to work history.

SENIOR TIP

You can find out how many credits you have earned by requesting your yearly Social Security Statement. (See page 2 for details on how to request this statement.)

SSD

You qualify for SSD if you can no longer do the type of work you had been doing and cannot do any other kind of work. Your disability must last or expect to last at least one year. If you qualify and have a spouse over age 62, he or she is also entitled to some benefits. You must have earned a certain number of Social Security work credits (it differs by age) to qualify.

To apply for this program, go in person to your local Social Security office. Bring the following items with you:

- your medical records;
- your social security number;
- your birth certificate;
- the names, addresses, and phone numbers of your doctors;
- a copy of your W-2 form; and,
- your most recent tax return.

You may be required to be examined by a doctor selected by the *Disability Determination Service* (a branch of Social Security). If your application is denied, you have sixty days to appeal. If approved, benefits begin in the sixth month of your disability. If you get benefits for two years, you are automatically enrolled in Medicare. Your case may be periodically reviewed to be sure you are still disabled.

It is possible to work and receive benefits. One program allows you to work on a trial basis for nine months while keeping your benefits in place. Then you can work for thirty-six months as long as your earnings are not substantial. (In 2004, earnings of more than $804 per month were considered *substantial*.) Once your benefits stop because you are working, there is a five year period in which the benefits can automatically start again, if you stop working.

SSI

Supplemental Security Income (SSI) is for people who are over age 65 and/or people who are disabled (so if you are disabled, you may be eligible before you are 65) and meet income requirements. Disability is defined as a physical or mental condition that prevents you from working.

To qualify, you must meet certain income guidelines (usually you cannot earn over $800 a month) and not own property worth more than $2000. This does not include your home, your car, burial plots, life insurance, and burial funds.

To qualify for SSI benefits, you must apply in person at your local office or call 800-772-1213. Bring the following items with you:

- your social security number;
- your birth certificate;
- information about your bank accounts, assets, and property; and,
- contact information for your doctors.

Appeals and Overpayments

The appeals process for SSI is the same as it is for Social Security retirement benefits. (see page 5.) If you should ever receive a notice about overpayment (that SSI paid you too much by mistake) do not panic. If the overpayment was not your fault and you are unable to pay it back—you may not have to do so. However, if this is the case, you must file a waiver with your local office (they will help you file). Otherwise, you would follow the standard appeals process. If it was your fault, you can pay it back gradually by having your payment reduced by $10 a month.

State Benefits

Only California, Hawaii, New Jersey, New York, and Rhode Island provide state disability payments. If you live in one of these states, check with your state labor department for more information.

Private Disability Policies

Many employers carry disability insurance policies that cover their employees. If you become disabled, check with your human resource department contact to determine if there is coverage and if so, how to apply.

GUARDIANSHIP

Should you ever reach a point in your life where you are unable to make decisions for yourself, a family member might seek *guardianship*. This occurs when a court appoints someone else to make decisions and handle finances for a person who is no longer mentally able to do so for themselves. Should someone seek guardianship of you, they must file a petition with the court; you must receive written notice; and, you have the right to a hearing in which you mental capacity can be determined. It is likely the court will appoint an attorney to represent you. You always have the right to appeal any decision made against you.

NOTE: Conservatorship *is slightly different and usually applies only to finances.*

–11–

VETERAN'S RIGHTS

A *veteran* is anyone who has served in the armed services, including the Reserve or National Guard. You must be honorably discharged to qualify for benefits. There is a wide array of benefits available to veterans. This chapter describes veteran's benefits and how to apply for them. The forms that are mentioned in this chapter are Veterans' Affairs (VA) documents and are available on their website at **www.va.gov** or at your local VA office.

DISABILITY COMPENSATION

Veterans who were injured while on active duty or whose condition was made worse by active duty are eligible for disability payments. To apply, use *VA Form 21-526, Veterans Application for Compensation or Pension.*

DISABILITY PENSION

A veteran's disability pension is paid to wartime veterans who can no longer work and who have limited income. You can view income charts online at **www.vba.va.gov/bln/21/Milsvc/Docs/Pensoneg.doc** to determine eligibility. To apply, use *VA Form 21-526, Veteran's Application for Compensation or Pension.*

NOTE: *Your veteran's benefits can reduce the amount of your SSD or SSI payments.*

DEPENDENCY AND INDEMNITY COMPENSATION

Dependency and indemnity compensation is a monthly benefit that is paid to the spouse of a veteran who died while on active duty; died from a service related injury; or, was receiving disability compensation for a service-related disability. The basic monthly payment rate is $967. You can apply at your local Veterans' Affairs office using *VA Form 21-534, Application for Dependency and Indemnity Compensation or Death Pension and Accrued Benefits by a Surviving Spouse or Child.*

DEATH PENSION BENEFIT

A *death pension benefit* is payable to the surviving spouse of a wartime veteran whose yearly income is under $6634 ($8109 if the surviving spouse is housebound). Apply using *VA Form 21-534, Application for Dependency and Indemnity Compensation or Death Pension by Surviving Spouse or Child.*

BURIAL PLOT ALLOWANCES

For a nonservice-related death (not occurring during service), the VA will provide reimbursement for burial and funeral expenses if the veteran died due to a service-related injury and was receiving VA benefits at the time of death (or was eligible to receive it) or died in a VA hospital, VA nursing home, or VA-approved state nursing home. Benefits include $300 for burial and funeral and $300 for plot-interment. Apply using *VA Form 21-530, Application for Burial Allowance.*

BURIAL FLAG

Free burial flags to drape over a coffin are provided for any veteran who was honorably discharged. Flags can be obtained at any post office or VA office. Apply *using VA Form 2008, Application for United States Flag for Burial Purposes.* (*VA Form 2008* provides the correct method for displaying and folding the flag.)

POW BENEFITS

Veterans who were POWs receive additional health benefits. Certain disorders and conditions have been determined to be service-related and include things like ulcers, cirrhosis, irritable bowel syndrome, and more. These veterans are eligible for VA health care as a result of these conditions.

LOAN GUARANTEES

Veterans are eligible for home loan guarantees up to $60,000. These guarantees can be used on manufactured homes, condos, lots for manufactured homes, to refinance a loan, or for traditional home purchases. To apply, use *VA Form 26-1880*.

HEALTH BENEFITS

If you are an honorably discharged veteran, you can apply for health benefits through the Veterans' Affairs Department. There is now a tiered system used to provide some veterans with free care while others must pay premiums. You can apply online and get more information at **www.va.gov/elig** or contact your local VA office.

OTHER BENEFITS

Other benefits that are available include life insurance, rehabilitation, and educational assistance. For more information, contact your local VA office.

SENIOR TIP

To find your local Veterans' Affairs office, visit:

www.va.gov/partners/stateoffice

or check the government section of your phone book.

–12–

LEGAL ASSISTANCE

Many people are simply not aware of what their rights are, how to get information, or how to find help. There is a wealth of information available to you—you just have to know how to find it. Additionally, there is free legal assistance available for seniors who qualify, but again, you have to know how to find it.

There are many places to go to get information about your rights and about programs that can benefit you. One good place to start is with your area's agency on aging. Check your phone book for contact information or contact the national office at:

Administration on Aging
200 Independence Avenue, S.W.
Washington, DC 20201
202-619-0257
www.aoa.gov

This agency is dedicated to the needs and rights of seniors, and if they cannot help you, they will be able to tell you who can.

Your local library is also a good source of information. If you are not sure where to find information, ask the

SENIOR TIP

The federal government has a website set up just to help seniors find government information. It is called *First Gov for Seniors* and is located at **www.seniors.gov**

librarian. Additionally, public libraries have computers with Internet access that you can often use for free. You may also be able to take a free course there that will teach you how to use a computer or the Internet if you do not know how.

Another important resource for seniors is AARP. Even if you are not an AARP member—and membership does have its benefits—its website is one of the most comprehensive for seniors. Contact them at:

AARP
601 E. Street NW
Washington, DC 20049
888-687-2277
www.aarp.org

FREE LEGAL ASSISTANCE

The *Older Americans Act* established funding for statewide legal hotlines to assist seniors ages 60 and up. The phone advice is free, but there is sometimes a small fee if the matter is referred to an attorney. Hotlines are listed in Appendix D.

All states provide some funding for free legal assistance clinics to seniors ages 60 and up. Access the list of clinics in Appendix C. To find a legal aid clinic in your area, check the list of programs online at **www.tcsg.org/lslinks.htm** or contact your local agency on aging. Additionally, some law schools maintain free legal assistance clinics for seniors. Contact your local law school to learn if anything is available. Depending on your income, you may also qualify for assistance from a legal aid society, which provides legal assistance to people who meet certain income requirements.

PENSION RIGHTS

The *Administration on Aging* provides funding for a pension-rights project that helps seniors obtain and receive pension benefits. The project has set up pension rights centers in the following locations:

EASTERN

Connecticut	888-425-6067
Maine	888-425-6067
Massachusetts	888-425-6067
Boston	617-287-7307
	www.pensionaction.org
New Hampshire	888-425-6067
Rhode Island	888-425-6067
Vermont	888-425-6067
New York	212-391-0120 ext. 17

CENTRAL

Southern Illinois	314-725-1516
	www.owlstlouis.com
Chicago	312-745-4430
	www.elderslaw.org/pension
Michigan	800-347-5297
Lansing	517-372-5959
	www.elderslaw.org/pension
Minnesota	651-645-0261 ext. 110; or ext.149
	www.mnseniors.org
Missouri	314-725-1516
	www.owlstlouis.com
Ohio	513-345-4160
	www.proseniors.org
Wisconsin	608-224-0660
	www.cwag.org/elder_law_center.htm

WESTERN

Arizona	520-790-7262
	www.pcoa.org
California	415-474-5171
	www.canhr.org

Assistance with company and union pensions is available through:

U.S. Department of Labor
Employee Benefits Security Administration
Inquiries: 866-444-EBSA (3272)
Publications: 800-998-7542
www.dol.gov/ebsa

Help with federal and civil service pensions is available at
Federal Civil Service Pensions:
U.S. Office of Personnel Management
Retirement: 888-767-6738; 202-606-0500
Thrift Savings (automated): 504-255-8777
www.opm.gov/retire

Railroad Pensions:
Railroad Retirement Board
Info & Field Office Locator
800-808-0772
www.rrb.gov

Military Pensions:
Defense Finance and Accounting Service
Retired and Annuitant Pay
800-321-1080
www.dfas.mil/money/retired

Pension Lawyer Referrals:
National Pension Lawyers Network
888-425-6067
www.pensionaction.org

ATTORNEY REFERRAL PROGRAMS

If you do not qualify for free or reduced fee legal assistance, you may wish to contact your state or local bar association's referral program. These programs refer you to an attorney in your area who is experienced in the area of law you need assistance with. For a referral to a member attorney in your area, you can also contact:

National Academy of Elder Law Attorneys, Inc.
1604 North Country Club Rd.
Tucson, Arizona 85716
520-881-4005
www.naela.com

AARP has a *Legal Counsel for the Elderly* program that can assist you in locating an attorney in your area and accessing free or low cost legal assistance for those who qualify. You can contact the AARP regarding this program at 202-434-2152 or online at **www.aarp.org**

Choosing an Attorney

If you are in a position in which you are selecting an attorney that you will pay, you want to make sure you choose someone you are comfortable with and who is experienced in the area of law you need help with. Remember that you will be paying this attorney, so you want to be sure you hire someone you like, you trust, and who will get you a good result for your dollar. Do not be intimidated by attorneys you meet with. Remember that you are the one calling the shots and you should only choose someone that inspires your confidence. Feel free to take a family member or friend along with you to meetings with attorneys.

Make an appointment for a free consultation and ask the attorney these questions.

- How long have you practiced law?
- How long have you practiced this specialty area of law?
- How many cases in this area have you handled in the past year?
- What are your fees?
- Do you handle this kind of case on a contingency fee basis?
- Are payment plans available?
- How much do you estimate my case will cost in total?
- What are my chances of winning?
- What kind of information will you need from me to handle this case?
- How long do you anticipate the case will take?
- Can you provide references?

After you have met with the attorney, ask yourself these questions.

- Was the office easily accessible for me?
- Did I feel comfortable in the office and with the attorney?
- Do I trust the attorney?
- Was the office staff friendly and pleasant?
- Did I wait longer than I would have liked?
- Did the attorney seem to understand my legal problem and see a clear course of action to solve it?
- Can I afford the legal bills that will result from the case?

Make sure that when you hire an attorney, you get a written retainer agreement or retainer letter specifically laying out costs and payment.

EPILOGUE

The first step to protecting your rights is understanding them, and hopefully this book has given you the information you need to help you recognize your rights. Fully understanding the benefits available to you will help you better access them and make the most of them.

This book will serve as a valuable reference as you face decisions and situations in the future and you can return to it again and again as you need answers.

GLOSSARY

A

administrator. Person who distributes the assets in an estate that does not have a will.

adult protective services. State agency that investigates elder abuse.

ALJ. An administrative law judge who hears a Medicaid appeal.

annuity. A financial arrangement where a bank pays a yearly sum in exchange for equity interest in a home.

appeal. To ask a court to decide that another court's decision was wrong.

assisted living. A facility in which assistance is provided with the activities of daily life.

B

beneficiary. A person who receives something from a will.

C

community property. Type of property distribution law that gives each spouse half of the marital assets.

community spouse resource amount. An amount the spouse of a person receiving Medicaid may keep as assets.

continuing care community. A long-term living choice that provides all levels of care for residents from senior living to skilled nursing care.

cremation. The process in which a body is turned to ash.

custodial care facility. An assisted-living facility.

D

DNR. A *do not resuscitate order* entered into a person's hospital record at their direction so they will not be resuscitated if their heart fails or they stop breathing.

E

equitable distribution. Type of property distribution law that distributes marital assets based on fairness.

estate. A legal term for everything a deceased person owned.

executor. A person chosen by the deceased to distribute the estate.

exempt assets. Assets that are not considered when you apply for Medicaid.

F

family council. A group of family members' of nursing home residents who meet to discuss issues and problems at the home.

H

health-care directive. A document giving someone else the power to make medical decisions for you or directing what kind of care you are willing accept.

health-care proxy. A legal document giving someone else the authority to make health-care decisions for you if you are unable to do so for yourself.

home equity conversion mortgage. A reverse mortgage in which the financial institution pays a lump sum.

home health-care aide. A worker trained to assist people with bathing, meal preparation, and household tasks.

hospice. A special care program for people with terminal illnesses.

I

intestate. Dying without a will.

L

living will. A legal document describing what type of medical care and intervention a person authorizes for him- or herself.

long-term care insurance. Private insurance that pays for nursing home care.

look back period. The thirty-six months before you apply for Medicaid from which all financial records must be provided to help determine eligibility.

licensed practical nurse (LPN). A nurse who has some medical training.

living benefits. Life insurance that pays a benefit while you are alive.

M

manufactured home. Trailer home.

mediation. A process through which you can resolve a case without going to court.

Medicare. Federally-funded health insurance for seniors.

Medicaid. A federally-funded health insurance program for low income people, which is managed by the states.

Medicaid annuity. A method by which you sell your home and invest the proceeds in an annuity that does not affect your Medicaid eligibility.

Medigap. Private health insurance that covers things Medicare does not.

N

nonexempt assets. Assets that must be considered when applying for Medicaid.

nursing home. A facility in which medical care is received on a long-term basis.

negligence. Failure to exercise the appropriate degree of care.

O

obituary. A death notice in a newspaper.

ombudsman. A state representative who handles complaints and inquiries about nursing homes.

P

plan of care. Plan describing how a nursing home resident will be cared for.

power of attorney. A legal document giving someone else authority to handle your financial affairs.

predatory lending. Mortgage lending that has high fees, high interest rates, and difficult terms.

prenuptial agreement. A contract made before marriage that determines each spouse's rights to property, in the event of a divorce.

private-duty nurse. A nurse employed by the patient and not the hospital or facility the patient is in.

probate. A court process in which a will is validated and then followed.

property tax exemption. A reduction in property tax.

Q

qualified Medicare beneficiary program. A state-sponsored program that pays Medicare premiums and co-pays.

R

release. A legal form that allows a doctor to share a patient's medical information with another person.

representative payee. A person authorized to receive benefits on your behalf from Social Security should you be unable to manage your own affairs.

resident council. A group of nursing home patients who meet to discuss issues and problems associated with the nursing home.

reverse mortgage. An arrangement where a financial institution gets title to a home and in return makes monthly or lump sum payments to the homeowner.

registered nurse (RN). A nurse who is able to administer medication and perform some medical procedures.

S

Section 8. Federal housing assistance.

senior living. Apartments for seniors that may have special medical alert systems and activity programs.

skilled nursing facility. A nursing home.

springing power of attorney. A power of attorney that becomes effective only upon the happening of an event named in it.

summary plan description. Description of a pension or retirement plan that lays out all the details of the plan.

T

testamentary trust. A trust created by a will.

Totten trust. A pay on death bank account.

trust. A legal entity that holds assets for another person.

V

veteran's benefits. Health-insurance benefits provided to honorably discharged military personnel.

vial of life. A program run by many sheriff departments, where a person keeps a vial on the refrigerator with health information and emergency contact information.

viatical settlement. A way to cash in a life insurance policy while you are alive

W

will. A legal document determining how your assets will be distributed after your death.

—Appendix A—

ORGANIZATIONS

AARP

601 E Street NW
Washington, DC 20049
800-424-3410
www.aarp.org

American Association of Homes and Services for the Aging (AAHSA)

2519 Connecticut Avenue, NW
Washington, DC 20008-1520
202-783-2242
www.aahsa.org

American Society on Aging

833 Market Street, Suite 512
San Francisco, CA 94103
415-882-2910
www.asaging.org

Assisted Living Federation of America (ALFA)

11200 Waples Mill Road
Fairfax, VA 22030
703-691-8100
www.alfa.org

The Centers for Medicare and Medicaid Services

7500 Security Boulevard
Baltimore, MD 21244
800-MEDICARE
www.medicare.gov

Clearinghouse on Abuse and Neglect of the Elderly (CANE)
University of Delaware
Department of Consumer Studies

Newark, DE 19716
302-831-3525
www.elderabusecenter.org

Department of Health and Human Services

200 Independence Avenue, SW
Washington, DC 20201
877-696-6775
www.dhhs.gov

Department of Housing and Urban Development (HUD)
HUD for Seniors

451 7th Street SW
Washington, DC 20410
202-708-1112
www.hud.gov/groups/seniors.cfm

Department of Labor
Employment and Training Administration
Division of Older Worker Programs

200 Constitution Avenue NW, Room N-4641
Washington, DC 20210
877-US-2JOBS
http://wdsc.doleta.gov/seniors

Department of Veterans Affairs (VA)

810 Vermont Avenue, NW
Washington, DC 20420
800-827-1000
www.va.gov

Gerontological Society of America

1275 K Street, NW
Suite 350
Washington, DC 20005-4006
202-842-1275
www.geron.org

Meals on Wheels

1414 Prince Street, Suite 302
Alexandria, VA 22314
703-548-5558
www.mowaa.org

Medic Alert

2323 Colorado Avenue
Turlock, CA 95382
888-633-4298
www.medicalert.org

Medicare Beneficiaries Defense Fund

1460 Broadway
Eighth Floor
New York, NY 10036-7393
212-869-3850
www.medicarerights.org

National Academy of Elder Law Attorneys, Inc.

1604 North Country Club Road
Tucson, Arizona 85716
520-881-4005
www.naela.com

National Association of Area Agencies on Aging
927 15th Street NW 6th Floor
Washington, DC 20005
202-296-8130
www.n4a.org

National Association for Home Care
228 7th Avenue Street SE
Washington, DC 20003
202-547-7424
www.nahc.org

National Association for Hispanic Elderly
234 East Colorado Blvd
Pasadena, CA 91101
626-564-1988

National Association of Social Security Claimants Representatives
6 Prospect Street
Midland Park, NJ 07432-1691
800-431-2804
www.nosscr.org

National Association of State Units on Aging
1225 I Street, Suite 725
Washington, DC 20005
202-898-2578
www.nasua.org

National Caucus and Center on Black Aged
1424 K Street, NW, Suite 500
Washington, DC 20005
202-637-8400
www.ncba-aged.org

National Center for Assisted Living
1201 L Street, NW
Washington, DC 20005
202-842-4444
www.ncal.org

National Center on Elder Abuse
1201 15th Street NW
Suite 350
Washington, DC 20005
212-898-2586
www.elderabusecenter.org

National Citizens' Coalition for Nursing Home Reform
1424 16th Street, NW, Suite 200
Washington, DC 20036-2211
www.nccnhr.org

National Council on Aging
100 D Street SW, Suite 801
Washington, DC 20024
202-479-1200
www.ncoa.org

National Funeral Director's Association
13625 Bishop's Drive
Brookfield, WI 53005-6607
414-541-2500
www.nfda.org

National Hispanic Council on Aging
2713 Ontario Road, NW
Washington, DC 20009
202-265-1288
www.nhcoa.org

National Hospice and Palliative Care Organization
1700 Diagonal Road, Suite 300
Alexandria, VA 22314
800-658-8898
www.nhpco.org

National Institute on Aging

Building 31, Room 5C27
31 Center Drive, MSC 2292
Bethesda, MD 20892
301-496-1752
www.nih.gov/nia

National Long-Term Care Resource Center
Division of Health Services
University of Minnesota School of Public Health

420 Delaware Street, SE
Minneapolis, MN 55455
612-624-5171
www.hsr.umn.edu

National Network of Estate Planning Attorneys

410 17th Street, Suite 1260
Denver, CO 80202
800-638-8681
www.netplanning.com

National Senior Citizen Law Center

1815 H Street, NW, Suite 700
Washington, DC 20006
202-887-5280
www.nsclc.org

Office of Civil Rights
Federal Transit Administration
U.S. Department of Transportation

400 Seventh Street, S.W., Room 9102
Washington, DC 20590
888-446-4511
www.fta.dot.gov

Office of Program Compliance and Disability Rights
Office of Fair Housing and Equal Opportunity
U.S. Department of Housing and Urban Development

451 7th Street, S.W., Room 5242
Washington, DC 20410
202-708-1112
www.hud.gov/offices/fheo/index.cfm

Older Women's League

1750 New York Ave. NW
Suite 350
Washington, DC 20006
202-783-6686
www.owl-national.org

Senior Community Service Employment Program (SCSEP)
AARP National Office

601 E Street NW
Washington DC 20049
202-434-2020
Locate a local office online at www.aarp.org/scsep-locate

Social Security Administration

6401 Security Blvd
Baltimore, MD 21235
800-772-1213
www.ssa.gov

State Long-Term Care Insurance Partnerships
University of Maryland Center of Aging

1240 HHP Building
College Park, MD 20742
301-405-7555
www.inform.umd.edu/aging/PLTC/index.html

U.S. Department of Justice
Civil Rights Division

950 Pennsylvania Avenue, NW
Disability Rights Section - NYAV
Washington, DC 20530
800-514-0301
www.usdoj.gov/crt/ada/adahom1.htm

Visiting Nurses Association of America

11 Beacon Street, Suite 910
Boston, MA 02108
888-866-8773
www.vnaa.org

—Appendix B—

WEB SITES

DRIVING

AAA Foundation for Traffic Safety's Senior Web Site

www.seniordrivers.org

ELDERCARE

Eldercare at Home

www.healthinaging.org

Eldercare Locator

www.eldercare.gov

EMPLOYMENT

Americans With Disabilities Act home page

www.usdoj.gov/crt/ada/adahom1.htm

AARP Best Employers for Seniors

www.aarp.org/bestemployers/

Benefits Check-up

www.benefitscheckup.org

Senior Job Bank

www.seniorjobbank.com

GENERAL

Ageline Database

www.research.aarp.org/ageline/home.html

Americans With Disabilities Act home page

www.usdoj.gov/crt/ada/adahom1.htm

Benefits Check-up

www.benefitscheckup.org

Carrier Alert Program

www.nalc.orgcommun/alert

Food Stamp Programs by State

www.cbpp.org/8-25-03fa.htm

National Council on Aging

www.noa.org

Senior Living

www.seniorliving.about.com

Senior Resource Directory

www.seniorresource.com

LEGAL

Americans with Disabilities Act

www.usdoj.gov/crt/ada/adahom1.htm

Elder Law Answers

www.elderlawanswers.com

First Gov for Seniors

www.firstgov.gov/Topics/seniors.shtml

Legal Aid Clinics

www.tcsg.org/lslinks.htm

MEDICARE/MEDICAID

Medicaid

www.cms.hhs.gov

Medicare

www.ssa.gov/mediinfo.htm

Medicare Participating Provider Physician Finder
www.medicare.gov/Physician/Home.asp

Medicare Participating Supplier Finder
www.medicare.gov/Supplier/Home.asp

Medicare Personal Plan Finder
www.medicare.gov/MPPF/Home.asp

Medicare Publications and Information Sheets
www.medicare.gov

Medicare State Contacts
www.medicare.gov/contacts/home.asp

Nursing Home Checklist
www.medicare.gov/nursing/checklist.asp

Nursing Home Inspection Reports and Comparisons
www.medicare.gov/Nhcompare/home.asp

Your Guide to Choosing a Nursing Home
www.medicare.gov/Publications/Pubs/pdf/nhguide.pdf

NURSING HOMES

Guide to Choosing a Nursing Home
www.pueblo.gsa.gov/cic_text/health/nursehme/nurshome.htm

Nursing Home Checklist
www.medicare.gov/nursing/checklist.asp

Nursing Home Inspection Reports and Comparisons
www.medicare.gov/Nursing/Overview.asp

Senior Living
www.seniorliving.about.com

Your Guide to Choosing a Nursing Home
www.medicare.gov/Publications/Pubs/pdf/nhguide.pdf

–Appendix C–

SENIOR LEGAL HOTLINE DIRECTORY

ARIZONA

Southern Arizona Legal Aid, Inc.
64 E. Broadway Blvd.
Tucson, AZ 85701
800-231-5441
520-623-5137

CALIFORNIA

Legal Services of Northern California
515 12th Street
Sacramento, CA 95814
800-222-1753
916-551-2140
www.seniorlegalhotline.org

CONNECTICUT

Connecticut Legal Services, Inc.
872 Main Street
PO Box 258
Willimantic, CT 06226
800-296-1467
www.ctelderlaw.org

DISTRICT OF COLUMBIA

Legal Counsel for the Elderly, AARP Foundation
601 E Street NW
Washington, DC 20049
202-434-2170

GEORGIA

Georgia Senior Legal Hotline
2 Peachtree Street Suite 9-398
Atlanta, GA 30303
888-257-9519
404-657-9915
www.gabar.org/senhot.asp

HAWAII

Legal Aid Society of Hawaii
924 Bethel Street
Honolulu, HI 96813-5119
888-536-0011
808-536-0011
www.legalaidhawaii.org

IOWA

Legal Hotline for Older Iowans
1111 9th Street Suite 230
Des Moines, IA 50314
800-992-8161
515-282-8161
www.iowalegalaid.org/hotline

IDAHO

Idaho Legal Aid Services
PO Box 913
310 North Fifth Street
Boise, Idaho 83701
866-345-0106
866-954-2591 (Spanish)
www.idaholegalaid.org

KANSAS

Kansas Legal Services
200 N. Broadway, Suite 500
Wichita, KS 67202
888-353-5337
316-265-9681
www.kansaslegalservices.org

KENTUCKY

Access to Justice Foundation
400 Old Vine Street, Suite 203
Lexington, KY 40507-1910
800-200-3633
www.accesstojustice.org

LOUISIANA

Southeast Louisiana Legal Services
1919 Common Street
New Orleans, LA 70112
504-529-1000
877-521-6242
www.nolac.org

MARYLAND

Legal Aid Bureau, Inc.
500 East Lexington Street
Baltimore, MD 21202
800-999-8904
410-539-5340
www.mdlab.org/srhotline.html

MAINE

Legal Services for the Elderly
9 Green Street
P.O. Box 2723
Augusta, ME 04338
800-750-5353
207-623-1797
www.mainelse.org

MICHIGAN

Elder Law Of Michigan, Inc.
222 N. Pine Street Suite 720
Lansing, MI 48933
800-347-5297
517-372-5959
www.elderslaw.org

NEW HAMPSHIRE

New Hampshire Legal Assistance
1361 Elm Street
Manchester, NH 03101
888-353-9944
603-624-6000
www.nhla.org

NEW MEXICO

State Bar of New Mexico Special Projects, Inc.
P.O. Box 25883
Albuquerque, NM 87125
800-876-6657
505-797-6005
www.nmbar.org

NORTH DAKOTA

Legal Services of North Dakota
P.O. Box 1666
Minot, ND 58702-1666
866-621-9886
www.legalassist.org

OHIO

Pro Seniors' Legal Hotline
7162 Reading Road Suite 1150
Cincinnati, OH 45237
800-488-6070
513-345-4160
www.proseniors.org

PENNSYLVANIA

Pennsylvania Senior Law HelpLine
100 South Broad Street
Philadelphia, PA 19110
877-727-7529
www.seniorlawcenter.org

SOUTH CAROLINA

South Carolina Centers for Equal Justice
1601-K Shop Road
Columbia, SC 29201
888-346-5592
www.centersforequaljustice.org

TEXAS

Texas Legal Services Center
815 Brazos, Suite 1100
Austin, TX 78701
800-622-2520
www.tlsc.org/hotline.html

WASHINGTON

Northwest Justice Project
401 Second Avenue South Suite 407
Seattle, WA 98104
888-387-7111
www.nwjustice.org

WEST VIRGINIA

West Virginia Senior Legal Aid
1988 Listravia Avenue
Morgantown, WV 26505
800-229-5068
304-291-3900
www.seniorlegalaid.org

WYOMING

Wyoming Legal Services

P.O. Box 1160

Lander, WY 82520

800-442-6710

307-332-6626

–Appendix D–

STATE-SPECIFIC RESOURCES

ALABAMA

Agency on Aging:	Alabama Dept. of Senior Services Montgomery, AL 36130 334-242-5743 www.aahha.org
Long-Term Care Ombudsman:	AL Dept. of Senior Services Montgomery, AL 36130 334-242-5743
Home/Hospice Care Organization:	Alabama Association of Home Health Agencies Montgomery, Alabama 36101 800-934-4312
Department of Public Health:	Alabama Department of Public Health www.alapubhealth.org
Elder Abuse Hotline Number:	800-458-7214

ALASKA

Agency on Aging:	Alaska Commission on Aging Juneau, AK 99811 907-465-3250
Long-Term Care Ombudsman:	AK Mental Health Trust Auth. Anchorage, AK 99501 907-334-4480

Home/Hospice Care Organization:	Alaska Home Care Association Anchorage, Alaska 99518 907-565-6100
Elder Abuse Hotline Numbers:	800-478-9996 907-269-3666

ARIZONA

Agency on Aging:	Aging and Adult Administration Phoenix, AZ 85007 602-542-4446
Long-Term Care Ombudsman:	AZ Aging & Adult Administration Phoenix, AZ 85007 602-542-6454
Home/Hospice Care Organization:	Arizona Association for Home Care Tempe, Arizona 85282 480-967-2624
Department of Public Health:	Arizona Dept. of Health Services www.hs.state.az.us
Elder Abuse Hotline Number:	877-767-2385

ARKANSAS

Agency on Aging:	Division Aging and Adult Services Little Rock, AR 72203 501-682-2441
Long-Term Care Ombudsman:	AR Division of Aging & Adult Services Little Rock, AR 72201-1437 501-682-8952
Home/Hospice Care Organization:	Home Care Association of AR Little Rock, AR 72201 501-682-8952
Department of Public Health:	Arkansas Dept. of Health http://healthyarkansas.com
Elder Abuse Hotline Numbers:	800-482-8049 800-582-4887

CALIFORNIA

Agency on Aging:	California Department of Aging Sacramento, CA 95814 916-322-5290
Long-Term Care Ombudsman:	CA Department on Aging Sacramento, CA 95814 916-322-3887
Home/Hospice Care Organization:	California Association for Health Servicesat Home Sacramento, California 95814 916-443-8055
Dept. of Public Health:	California Department of Health Services www.dhs.cahwnet.gov
Elder Abuse Hotline Numbers:	888-436-3600 800-231-4024

COLORADO

Agency of Aging:	Aging and Adult Services Denver, CO 80203 303-866-2800
Long-Term Care Ombudsman:	The Legal Center Denver, CO 80203 800-288-1376
Home/Hospice Care Organization:	Home Care Association of Colorado Englewood, Colorado 80112 303-694-4728
Dept. of Public Health:	Colorado Department of Public Health and Environment: www.state.co.us/gov_dir/cdphe_dir
Elder Abuse Hotline Numbers:	800-773-1366 800-866-7689

CONNECTICUT

Agency on Aging:	Division of Elderly Services Hartford, CT 06106-5033 860-424-5298
Long-Term Care Ombudsman:	CT Department of Social Services Hartford, CT 06106 860-424-5200
Home/Hospice Care Organization:	Connecticut Association for Home Care, Inc. Wallingford, Connecticut 06492 203-265-9931
Department of Public Health:	Connecticut Department of Health: www.state.ct.us/dph
Elder Abuse Hotline Numbers:	888-385-4225 860-424-5241

DELAWARE

Agency on Aging:	Delaware Division of Services for Aging and Adults with Physical Disabilities New Castle, DE 19720 302-577-4791
Long-Term Care Ombudsman:	Division of Services for Aging & Adults New Castle, DE 19720 302-577-4791
Home/Hospice Care Organization:	Home Health Corp of America Newark, Delaware 19711 800-333-4208 Delaware Hospice Association Wilmington, Delaware 19810
Elder Abuse Hotline Numbers:	800-838-9800 800-223-9074

DISTRICT OF COLUMBIA

Agency on Aging:	District of Columbia Office on Aging Washington, DC 20001 202-724-5622
Long-Term Care Ombudsman:	Legal Counsel for the Elderly Washington, DC 20049 202-434-2140
Home/Hospice Care Organization:	Maryland-National Capital Homecare Assn Alexandria, VA 22314 708-535-1885
Elder Abuse Hotline Numbers:	202-541-3950 202-434-2140

FLORIDA

Agency on Aging:	Department of Elder Affairs Tallahassee, FL 32399 850-414-2000
Long-Term Care Ombudsman:	Florida State LTC Ombudsman Council Tallahassee, FL 32301 888-831-0404
Home/Hospice Care Organization:	Associated Home Health Industries of Florida, Inc. Tallahassee, Florida 32301-2600 850-222-8967 Florida Hospital Association Orlando, Florida 32803 407-841-6230
Department of Public Health:	Florida Department of Health www.doh.state.fl.us
Elder Abuse Hotline Number:	800-962-2873

GEORGIA

Agency on Aging:	Division of Aging Services Atlanta, GA 30303 404-657-5258
Long-Term Care Ombudsman:	Office of the State LTCO Atlanta, GA 30303-3142 888-454-5826
Home/Hospice Care Organization:	Georgia Association for Comprehensive Home Care, Inc. Marietta, Georgia 30062 770-565-4531
Department of Public Health:	Georgia Division of Public Health: www.ph.dhr.state.ga.us
Elder Abuse Hotline Numbers:	404-657-5726 404-657-4076

HAWAII

Agency on Aging:	Hawaii Executive Office on Aging Honolulu, HI 96813 808-586-0100
Long-Term Care Ombudsman:	Executive Office on Aging Honolulu, HI 96813 808-586-0100
Home/Hospice Care Organization:	Home Care and Hospice Division, Healthcare Association of Hawaii Honolulu, Hawaii 96814 808-521-8961
Department of Public Health:	Hawaii Department of Health www.hawaii.gov/health
Elder Abuse Hotline Numbers:	808-832-5115 (Oahu) 808-243-5151 (Maui) 808-241-3432 (Kauai) 808-933-882 (East Hawaii) 808-327-6280 (West Hawaii)

IDAHO

Agency on Aging:	Idaho Commission on Aging Boise, ID 83720-0007 208-334-3833
Long-Term Care Ombudsman:	Idaho Commission on Aging Boise, ID 83720 208-334-2220
Home/Hospice Care Organization:	Idaho Association of Home Health Agencies Boise, Idaho 83707 208-362-8190
Department of Public Health:	Idaho Department of Health and Welfare www.state.id.us/dhw/hwgd_www/home.html
Elder Abuse Hotline Numbers:	208-334-3833 208-364-1899

ILLINOIS

Agency on Aging:	Illinois Department on Aging Springfield, IL 62701-1789 217-785-3356 Chicago Office: 312-814-2630 In-state toll free Senior HelpLine: 800-252-8966
Long-Term Care Ombudsman:	Illinois Department on Aging Springfield, IL 62701 217-785-3143
Home/Hospice Care Organization:	Illinois Home Care Council Glenview, Illinois 60025 847-657-6960 VNA First LaGrange, Illinois 60525 708-788-2047
Department of Public Health:	Illinois Department of Public Health: www.idph.state.il.us
Elder Abuse Hotline Numbers:	800-252-8966 800-252-4343

INDIANA

Agency on Aging:	Bureau of Aging and In-Home Services Indianapolis, IN 46207-7083 317-232-7020
Long-Term Care Ombudsman:	Indiana Division Disabilities Rehab Services Indianapolis, IN 46207 800-545-7763
Home/Hospice Care Organization:	Indiana Association for Home and Hospice Care, Inc. Indianapolis, Indiana 46250 317-844-6630
Department of Public Health:	Indiana State Department of Health www.in.gov/isdh
Elder Abuse Hotline Number:	800-992-6978

IOWA

Agency on Aging:	Iowa Department of Elder Affairs Des Moines, IA 50309-3609 515-242-3333
Long-Term Care Ombudsman:	Iowa Department of Elder Affairs Des Moines, IA 50309 515-242-3327
Home/Hospice Care Organization:	Iowa Association for Home Care Des Moines, Iowa 50309 515-282-3965 Iowa Hospice Organization Des Moines, Iowa 50309 515-243-1046
Department of Public Health:	Iowa Department of Health http://idph.state.ia.us
Elder Abuse Hotline Numbers:	800-362-2178 515-281-4115

KANSAS

Agency on Aging:	Department on Aging Topeka, KS 66603 785-296-4986
Long-Term Care Ombudsman:	Kansas Office of the State LTC Ombudsman Topeka, KS 66612 785-296-3017
Home/Hospice Care Organization:	Kansas Home Care Association Lawrence, KS 66047 785-841-8611 Association of Kansas Hospice Witchita, Kansas 67213 316-263-6380
Department of Public Health:	Kansas Department of Health and Environment www.ink.org/public/kdhe
Elder Abuse Hotline Numbers:	800-922-5330 785-296-0044 800-842-0078

KENTUCKY

Agency on Aging:	Office of Aging Services Frankfort, KY 40621 502-564-6930
Long-Term Care Ombudsman:	Office of Aging Services Frankfort, KY 40621 502-564-6930
Home/Hospice Care Organization:	Kentucky Home Health Association Lexington, KY 40517 859-268-2574
Elder Abuse Hotline Numbers:	800-752-6200 800-372-2991

LOUISIANA

Agency on Aging: Governor's Office of Elderly Affairs
Baton Rouge, LA 70898
225-342-7100

Long-Term Care Ombudsman: Office of Elderly Affairs
Baton Rouge, LA 70898
225-342-7100

Home/Hospice Care Organization: HomeCare Association of Louisiana
New Iberia, Louisiana 70562
337-560-9610

Elder Abuse Hotline Number: 800-259-4990

MAINE

Agency on Aging: Bureau of Elder and Adult Services
Augusta, ME 04333
207-624-5335

Long-Term Care Ombudsman: Maine LTC Ombudsman Program
Augusta, ME 04332
207-621-1079

Home/Hospice Care Organization: Home Care Alliance of Maine
Augusta, Maine 04330
207-623-0345

Elder Abuse Hotline Number: 800-624-8404

MARYLAND

Agency on Aging: Maryland Department of Aging
Baltimore, MD 21201-2374
410-767-1100

Long-Term Care Ombudsman: Maryland Department of Aging
Baltimore, MD 21201
410-767-1100

Home/Hospice Care Organization: Maryland-National Capital Homecare Association
Alexandria, Virginia 22314
703-535-1885

Department of Public Health: Maryland Department of Health and Mental Hygiene
www.mdpublichealth.org

Elder Abuse Hotline Number: 800-917-7383

MASSACHUSETTS

Agency on Aging: Massachusetts Executive Office of Elder Affairs
Boston, MA 02108
617-727-7750

Long-Term Care Ombudsman: Massachusetts Executive Office of Elder Affairs
Boston, MA 02108
617-727-7750

Home/Hospice Care Organization: Massachusetts Council for Home Care Aide Services
Boston, Massachusetts 02114
617-227-6641

Visiting Nurses Association of New England
Needham, Massachusetts 02194
781-444-0713

Department of Public Health: Massachusetts Department of Health
www.magnet.state.ma.us/dph/dphhome.htm

Elder Abuse Hotline Numbers: 800-922-2275
800-462-5540

MICHIGAN

Agency on Aging: Michigan Office of Services to the Aging
Lansing, MI 48909
517-373-8230

Long-Term Care Ombudsman: Elderlaw of Michigan
Lansing, MI 48933
866-485-9393

Home/Hospice Care Organization:	Michigan Home Health Association Okemos, Michigan 48864 517-349-8089
Department of Public Health:	Michigan Department of Public Health www.mdch.state.mi.us
Elder Abuse Hotline Numbers:	800-996-6228 800-882-6006

MINNESOTA

Agency on Aging:	Minnesota Board on Aging St. Paul, MN 55155-3843 651-296-2770
Long-Term Care Ombudsman:	Office of Ombudsman for Older Minnesotans St. Paul, MN 55101 800-657-3591
Home/Hospice Care Organization:	Minnesota HomeCare Association St. Paul, Minnesota 55113-4036 651-635-0607
Department of Public Health:	Minnesota Department of Public Health www.health.state.mn.us
Elder Abuse Hotline Number:	800-333-2433

MISSISSIPPI

Agency on Aging:	Division of Aging and Adult Services Jackson, MS 39202 601-359-4925
Long-Term Care Ombudsman:	MS Department of Human Services, Div. of Aging Jackson, MS 39202 601-359-4927
Home/Hospice Care Organization:	Mississippi Association for Home Care Ridgeland, MS 39158 601-853-7533

	Mississippi Hospital Association Jackson, Mississippi 39236 601-368-3220
Department of Public Health:	Mississippi Department of Health www.msdh.state.ms.us
Elder Abuse Hotline Numbers:	800-222-8000 800-227-7308

MISSOURI

Agency on Aging:	Division on Aging Jefferson City, MO 65102 573-751-3082
Long-Term Care Ombudsman:	Department of Health & Senior Services Jefferson City, MO 65102 800-309-3282
Home/Hospice Care Organization:	Missouri Alliance for Home Care Jefferson City, Missouri 65109 573-634-7772
	Missouri Hospital Home Health Council Jefferson City, Missouri 65102 573-893-3700
Department of Public Health:	Missouri Department of Health www.health.state.mo.us
Elder Abuse Hotline Number:	800-392-0210

MONTANA

Agency on Aging:	Senior and Long Term Care Division Helena, MT 59620 406-444-4077
Long-Term Care Ombudsman:	Montana Department of Health & Human Services Helena, MT 59604 406-444-4676

Home/Hospice Care Organization: Montana Association of Home Health Agencies
Missoula, Montana 59801
406-721-4035

Montana Hospital Association
Helena, Montana 59604
406-442-1911

Department of Public Health: Montana Department of Health
www.mt.gov

Elder Abuse Hotline Number: 800-332-2272

NEBRASKA

Agency on Aging: Division on Aging
Lincoln, NE 68509
402-471-2307

Long-Term Care Ombudsman: Division of Aging Services
Lincoln, NE 68509
402-471-2307

Home/Hospice Care Organization: Nebraska Association of Home and CommunityHealth Agencies
Lincoln, Nebraska 68516
402-489-1117

Department of Public Health: Nebraska Department of Health
www.hhs.state.ne.us

Elder Abuse Hotline Number: 800-652-1999

NEVADA

Agency on Aging: Nevada Division for Aging Services
Carson City, NV 89706
775-687-4210

Long-Term Care Ombudsman: Nevada Division for Aging Services
Reno, NV 89502
775-688-2964

Home/Hospice Care Organization: Home Health Care Assn of Nevada
Reno, Nevada 89502
775-982-5860

Elder Abuse Hotline Numbers: 800-992-5757
702-784-8090 (Reno area)

NEW HAMPSHIRE

Agency on Aging: Division of Elderly and Adult Services
Concord, NH 03301
603-271-4680

Long-Term Care Ombudsman: NH LTC Ombudsman Program
Concord, NH 03301
603-271-4375

Home/Hospice Care Organization: Home Care Association of New Hampshire
Concord, New Hampshire 03301
603-225-5597

Department of Public Health: New Hampshire Department of Health and Human Services
www.dhhs.state.nh.us/Index.nsf?open

Elder Abuse Hotline Numbers: 800-949-0470
603-271-4386
800-442-5640

NEW JERSEY

Agency on Aging: Department of Health and Senior Services
Trenton, New Jersey 08625-0807
609-943-3436
1-800-792-8820

Long-Term Care Ombudsman: Office of Ombudsman for Institutional Elderly
Trenton, NJ 08625
609-943-4026

Home/Hospice Care Organization: Home Health Assembly of New Jersey, Inc.
Princeton Junction, New Jersey 08550
609-275-6100

Home Care Council of New Jersey
Verona, New Jersey 07044
973-857-3333

New Jersey Hospital Association
Princeton, New Jersey 08543
609-275-4000

Department of Public Health: New Jersey Department of Health and Senior Services
www.state.nj.us/health

Elder Abuse Hotline Number: 800-792-8820

NEW MEXICO

Agency on Aging: State Agency on Aging
Santa Fe, NM 87501
505-827-7640

Long-Term Care Ombudsman: State LTC Ombudsman
Albuquerque, NM 87110
505-255-0971

Home/Hospice Care Organization: New Mexico Association for Home Care
Albuquerque, New Mexico 87110
505-889-4556

Department of Public Health: New Mexico Department of Health
www.health.state.nm.us/website.nsf/frames?readform

Elder Abuse Hotline Numbers: 800-797-3260
505-841-6100

NEW YORK

Agency on Aging:
New York State Office for the Aging
Albany, NY 12223
800-342-9871

Long-Term Care Ombudsman:
New York State Office for the Aging
Albany, NY 12223
518-474-7329

Home/Hospice Care Organization:
Home Care Association of
New York State, Inc.
Albany, New York 12210
518-426-8764

New York State Association of
Health Care Providers, Inc.
Albany, New York 12207
518-463-1118

Health Care Association of
New York State
Rensselaer, New York 12144
518-431-7600

Hospice and Palliative Care Assn
of New York State
Albany, New York 12205
518-446-1483

Home Care Council of New York City
New York, New York 10036
646-366-0860

Department of Public Health:
New York State Department of Health
www.health.state.ny.us

Elder Abuse Hotline Numbers:
800-342-9871
800-220-7184 (N. Eastern)
800-425-0314 (Buffalo)
800-837-9018 (Rochester)
800-425-0319 (Syracuse)
800-425-0316 (New York City)
800-425-0320 (L. Hudson Vly)
800-425-0323 (Long Island)

NORTH CAROLINA

Agency on Aging:
Department of Health and
Human Services
Raleigh, NC 27699
919-733-3983

Long-Term Care Ombudsman:
North Carolina Division of Aging
Raleigh, NC 27699
919-733-8395

Home/Hospice Care Organization:
Association for Home Care and Hospice
of North Carolina, Inc.
Raleigh, North Carolina 27609
919-848-3450

The Carolinas Center for Hospice and
End of Life Care
Raleigh, North Carolina 27609
919-878-1717

Department of Public Health:
North Carolina Department
of Public Health
www.dhhs.state.nc.us

Elder Abuse Hotline Number:
800-662-7030

NORTH DAKOTA

Agency on Aging:
Department of Human Services
Aging Services Division
Bismarck, ND 58504
800-451-8693

Long-Term Care Ombudsman:
Aging Services Division
Bismarck, ND 58504
800-451-8693

Home/Hospice Care Organization:
North Dakota Association
for Home Care
Bismarck, North Dakota 58502
701-224-1815

Department of Public Health: North Dakota Department of Health
www.ehs.health.state.nd.us/ndhd

Elder Abuse Hotline Number: 800-451-8693

OHIO

Agency on Aging: Ohio Department of Aging
Columbus, OH 43215-5928
614-466-5500

Long-Term Care Ombudsman: Ohio Department of Aging
Columbus, OH 43215
614-466-1221

Home/Hospice Care Organization: Ohio Council for Home Care
Columbus, Ohio 43229
614-885-0434

Ohio Hospice & Palliative Care Organization
Columbus, Ohio 43221
614-485-0021

Department of Public Health: Ohio Department of Health
www.odh.state.oh.us

Elder Abuse Hotline Numbers: 800-635-3748
800-282-1206

OKLAHOMA

Agency on Aging: Aging Services Division
Oklahoma City, OK 73125
405-521-2281 or 521-2327

Long-Term Care Ombudsman: Aging Services Division
OK Department
Oklahoma City, OK 73105
405-521-6734

Home/Hospice Care Organization: Oklahoma Association for Home Care
Oklahoma City, Oklahoma 73127
405-495-5995

Department of Public Health:	Oklahoma State Department of Health www.health.state.ok.us
Elder Abuse Hotline Number:	800-522-3511

OREGON

Agency on Aging:	Senior and Disabled Services Division Salem, OR 97301 503-945-5811
Long-Term Care Ombudsman:	Oregon Office of the LTC Ombudsman Salem, OR 97305 503-378-6533
Home/Hospice Care Organization:	Oregon Association for Home Care Salem, Oregon 97302 503-364-2733
Department of Public Health:	Oregon Department of Human Resources www.ohd.hr.state.or.us
Elder Abuse Hotline Number:	800-232-3020

PENNSYLVANIA

Agency on Aging:	Pennsylvania Department of Aging Harrisburg, PA 17101 717-783-1550
Long-Term Care Ombudsman:	Pennsylvania Department of Aging Harrisburg, PA 17101 717-783-7247
Home/Hospice Care Organization:	Pennsylvania Homecare Association Lemoyne, Pennsylvania 17043 717-975-9448
Department of Public Health:	Pennsylvania Department of Health http://webserver.health.state.pa.us/health/site
Elder Abuse Hotline Numbers:	800-490-8505 800-254-5164

PUERTO RICO

Agency on Aging: Governor's Office of Elderly Affairs
Old San Juan Station, PR 00902
787-721-5710

Long-Term Care Ombudsman: Puerto Rico Governor's
Office Elder Affairs
San Juan, PR 00902
787-725-1515

Home/Hospice Care Organization: Puerto Rico Home Health Agencies and
Hospices Association
Arecibo, PR 00614
787-879-2955

Elder Abuse Hotline Numbers: 787-725-9788
787-721-8225

RHODE ISLAND

Agency on Aging: Department of Elderly Affairs
Providence, RI 02903
401 222-2858

Long-Term Care Ombudsman: Alliance for Better Long Term Care
Warwick, RI 02888
401-785-3340

Home/Hospice Care Organization: Rhode Island Partnership for
Home Care, Inc.
Providence, Rhode Island 02906
401-751-2487

Department of Public Health: Rhode Island Department of Health
www.health.state.ri.us

Elder Abuse Hotline Numbers: 401-462-0550
401-785-3340

SOUTH CAROLINA

Agency on Aging: Office of Senior and
Long Term Care Services
Columbia, SC 29202
803-898-2501

Long-Term Care Ombudsman:	SC DHHS, Office Aging Columbia, SC 29202 803-898-2850
Home/Hospice Care Organization:	South Carolina Home Care Association Columbia, South Carolina 29202 803-254-7355
	Hospice for the Carolinas West Columbia, South Carolina 29171-6009 803-791-4220
Department of Public Health:	South Carolina Department of Health and Environmental Control www.state.sc.us:80/dhec
Elder Abuse Hotline Numbers:	800-898-7318 800-898-2850

SOUTH DAKOTA

Agency on Aging:	Office of Adult Services and Aging Pierre, SD 57501 605-773-3656
Long-Term Care Ombudsman:	SD Office of Adult Services & Aging Pierre, SD 57501 605-773-3656
Home/Hospice Care Organization:	South Dakota Association of Healthcare Organizations Sioux Falls, South Dakota 57106 605-361-2281
Department of Public Health:	South Dakota Department of Health www.state.sd.us/state/executive/ doh/doh.html
Elder Abuse Hotline Number:	605-773-3656

TENNESSEE

Agency on Aging:	Commission on Aging and Disability Nashville, Tennessee 37243 615-741-2056
Long-Term Care Ombudsman:	TN Commission on Aging and Disability Nashville, TN 37243 615-741-2056
Home/Hospice Care Organization:	Tennessee Association for Home Care, Inc. Nashville, Tennessee 37214 615-885-3399 Tennessee Hospital Association Home Care Alliance Nashville, Tennessee 37210 615-256-8240
Department of Public Health:	Tennessee Department of Health www.state.tn.us/health
Elder Abuse Hotline Number:	888-277-8366

TEXAS

Agency on Aging:	Texas Department on Aging Austin, TX 78751 512-424-6840
Long-Term Care Ombudsman:	Texas Department on Aging Austin, TX 78711 512-424-6875
Home/Hospice Care Organization:	Texas Association for Home Care 3737 Executive Center Drive Austin, Texas 78731 512-338-9293
Department of Public Health:	Texas Department of Health www.tdh.texas.gov
Elder Abuse Hotline Numbers:	512-834-3784 800-252-5400 512-438-2633 800-458-9858

UTAH

Agency on Aging:	Division of Aging & Adult Services Salt Lake City, UT 84145 801-538-3910
Long-Term Care Ombudsman:	Utah Division of Aging & Adult Services Salt Lake City, UT 84103 801-538-3924
Home/Hospice Care Organization:	Utah Association of Home Health Agencies Midvale, Utah 84047 801-255-5888
Department of Public Health:	Utah Department of Health http://hlunix.ex.state.ut.us
Elder Abuse Hotline Numbers:	801-264-7669 800-371-7897

VERMONT

Agency on Aging:	Vermont Department of Aging and Disabilities Waterbury, VT 05671 802-241-2400
Long-Term Care Ombudsman:	Vermont Legal Aid, Inc. Burlington, VT 05402 802-863-5620
Home/Hospice Care Organization:	Vermont Assembly of Home Health Agencies Montpelier, Vermont 05602 802-229-0579
Elder Abuse Hotline Number:	800-564-1612

VIRGINIA

Agency on Aging:
Virginia Department for the Aging
Richmond, VA 23229
804-662-9333

Long-Term Care Ombudsman:
Virginia Association Area Agencies on Aging
Richmond, VA 23219
804-644-2804

Home/Hospice Care Organization:
Virginia Association for Home Care
Richmond, Virginia 23226
800-755-8636

Virginia Hospital and Health Care Association
Richmond, Virginia 23294
804-965-1249

Department of Public Health:
Virginia Department of Health
www.vdh.state.va.us

Elder Abuse Hotline Numbers:
888-832-3858
804-371-0896

WASHINGTON

Agency on Aging:
Aging and Adult Services Administration
Olympia, WA 98504
360-725-2310
In-state only: 800-422-3263

Long-Term Care Ombudsman:
South King County Multi-Service Center
Federal Way, WA 98093
253-838-6810

Home/Hospice Care Organization:
Home Care Association of Washington
Edmonds, Washington 98020
425-775-8120

Department of Public Health:
Washington State Department of Health
www.doh.wa.gov

Elder Abuse Hotline Numbers:
800-422-3263
800-562-6078

WEST VIRGINIA

Agency on Aging:	West Virginia Bureau of Senior Services Charleston, WV 25305 304-558-3317
Long-Term Care Ombudsman:	West Virginia Bureau of Senior Services Charleston, WV 25302 304-558-3317
Home/Hospice Care Organization:	West Virginia Council of Home Care Agencies, Inc. Middlebourne WV 26149 304-758-4312
Elder Abuse Hotline Number:	800-352-6513

WISCONSIN

Agency on Aging:	Bureau of Aging and Long Term Care Resources Madison, WI 53707 608-266-2536
Long-Term Care Ombudsman:	Wisconsin Board on Aging & Long Term Care Madison, WI 53703 608-266-8945
Home/Hospice Care Organization:	Wisconsin Homecare Organization Madison, Wisconsin 53719 608-278-1115
Department of Public Health:	Wisconsin Department of Health and Family Services www.dhfs.state.wi.us
Elder Abuse Hotline Numbers:	608-266-2536 800-815-0015 608-246-7013

WYOMING

Agency on Aging:	Division on Aging Cheyenne, WY 82002 307-777-7986
Long-Term Care Ombudsman:	Wyoming Senior Citizens, Inc Wheatland, WY 82201 307-322-5553
Home/Hospice Care Organization:	Home Health Care Alliance of Wyoming Casper, WY 82601 307-237-7042
Department of Public Health:	Wyoming Department of Health http://wdhfs.state.wy.us/WDH
Elder Abuse Hotline Numbers:	307-777-6137 307-777-7123

–Appendix E–

NURSING HOME RESIDENT'S RIGHTS IN THE U.S.

BACKGROUND

The following Residents' Rights must be adhered to by all nursing homes in the United States that wish to participate in the government's Medicare or Medicaid program. For further information, contact:

Centers for Medicare & Medicaid Services
7500 Security Blvd.
Baltimore, MD 21244-1850
410-786-6778

NURSING HOME RESIDENTS' RIGHTS IN THE UNITED STATES

As a resident of this facility, you have the right to a dignified existence and to communicate with individuals and representatives of choice. The facility will protect and promote your rights as designated below.

Exercise of Rights—

You have the right and freedom to exercise your rights as a resident of this facility and as a citizen or resident of the United States without fear of discrimination, restraint, interference, coercion or reprisal. If you are unable to act in your own behalf, your rights are exercised by the person appointed under state law to act in your behalf.

Notice of Rights and Services—

You will be informed of your rights and of all rules and regulations governing resident conduct and responsibilities both orally and in writing.

You have the right to inspect and purchase photocopies of your records.

You have the right to be fully informed of your total health status.

You have the right to refuse treatment and the right to refuse to participate in experimental research.

You have the right to formulate an advance directive in accordance with facility policy.

You will be informed of Medicare and Medicaid benefits. This information will be posted.

You will be informed of facility services and charges.

The facility will inform you of procedures for protecting personal funds. If you deem necessary, you may file a complaint with the state survey and certification agency.

You will be informed of your physician, his or her specialty, and ways of contacting him or her.

The facility must consult with you and notify your physician and interested family members of any significant change in your condition or treatment, or of any decision to transfer or discharge.

The facility will notify you and interested family members of a room or roommate change.

You have the right to refuse room changes requested by the facility.

The facility will periodically update the address and telephone number of your legal representative or interested family members.

The facility will notify you and interested family members of change in your rights as a resident.

Protection of Funds—

You may manage your own financial affairs. You are not required to deposit personal funds with the facility.

The facility must manage your deposited funds with your best interests in mind. Your money will not be commingled with facility funds.

The facility will provide you with an individualized financial report quarterly and upon your request.

Any remaining estate will be conveyed to your named successor.

All funds held by the facility will be protected by a security bond.

Free Choice—

You may choose your own personal physician.

You will be informed of and may participate in your care and treatment and any resulting changes.

Privacy—

You have the right of privacy over your personal and clinical records.

Your privacy will include: personal care, medical treatments, telephone use, visits, letters, and meetings of family and resident groups.

You may approve or refuse the release of your records except in the event of a transfer or legal situation.

Grievances—

You may voice grievances concerning your care without fear of discrimination or reprisal.

You may expect prompt efforts for the resolution of grievances.

Examination of Survey Results—

You may examine survey results and the plan of correction. These, or a notice of their location, will be posted in a readily accessible place.

You may contact client advocate agencies and receive information from them.

Work—

You may perform or refuse to perform services for the facility. All services performed must be well documented in the care plan to include the nature of the work and compensation.

Mail—

You may promptly send and receive your mail unopened and have access to writing supplies.

Access and Visitation Rights—

You have the right to receive or deny visitors.

You have the right and the facility must provide access to visit with any relevant agency of the state or any entity providing health, social, legal or other services.

Telephone—

You have the right to use the telephone in private.

Personal Property—

You can retain and use personal possessions as space permits.

Married Couples—

A married couple may share a room.

Self-Administration of Drugs—

You may self-administer drugs unless determined unsafe by the interdisciplinary team.

ADMISSION, TRANSFER AND DISCHARGE RIGHTS

Transfer and Discharge—

You may not be transferred or discharged unless your needs cannot be met, safety is endangered, services are no longer required, or payment has not been made.

Notice of and reason(s) for transfer or discharge must be provided to you in an understandable manner.

Notice of transfer or discharge must be given 30 days prior, except in case of health and safety needs.

The transfer or discharge notice must include the name, address and telephone number of the appropriate, responsible protective agency.

A facility must provide sufficient preparation to ensure a safe transfer or discharge.

Notice of Bed-Hold Policy and Readmission—

You and a family member must receive written notice of state and facility bed-hold policies before and at the time of a transfer.

The facility must follow a written policy for readmittance if the bed-hold period is exceeded.

Equal Access to Quality Care—

The facility must use identical policies regarding transfer, discharge and services for all residents.

The facility may determine charges for a nonMedicaid resident as long as written notice was provided at the time of admission.

Admission Policy—

The facility must not require a third party guarantee of payment or accept any gifts as a condition of admission or continued stay.

This facility cannot require you to waive your right to receive or apply for Medicare or Medicaid benefits.
The facility may obtain legal financial access for payment without incurring your personal liability.
The facility may charge a Medicaid-eligible resident for items and services requested.
The facility may only accept contributions if they are not a condition of admission or continued stay.

RESIDENT BEHAVIOR AND FACILITY PRACTICES

Restraints—

The facility may not use physical restraints or psychoactive drugs for discipline or convenience or when they are not required to treat medical symptoms.

Abuse—

You have the right to be free from verbal, sexual, physical or mental abuse, corporal punishment and involuntary seclusion.

Staff Treatment—

The facility must implement procedures that protect you from abuse, neglect or mistreatment, and misappropriation of your property.
In the event of an alleged violation involving your treatment, the facility is required to report it to the appropriate officials.
All alleged violations must be thoroughly investigated and the results reported.

Quality of Life—

The facility must care for you in a manner that enhances your quality of life.

Dignity—

The facility will treat you with dignity and respect in full recognition of your individuality.

Self Determination—

You may choose your own activities, schedules and health care and any other aspect affecting your life within the facility.

You may interact with visitors of your choice.

Participation in Resident and Family Groups—

You may organize or participate in groups of choice.

Families have the right to visit with other families.

The facility must provide a private space for group meetings.

Staff or visitors may attend meetings at the group's invitation.

The facility will provide a staff person to assist and follow up with the group's requests.

The facility must listen to and act upon requests or concerns of the group.

Participation in Other Activities—

You have the right to participate in activities of choice that do not interfere with the rights of other residents.

Accommodation of Needs—

You have the right as a resident to receive services with reasonable accommodations to individual needs and preferences.

You will be notified of room or roommate changes.

You have the right to make choices about aspects of your life in the facility that are important to you.

Activities—

The facility will provide a program of activities designed to meet your needs and interests.

Social Services—

The facility will provide social services to attain or maintain your highest level of well-being.

Environment—

The facility must provide a safe, clean, comfortable, home-like environment, allowing you the opportunity to use your personal belongings to the extent possible.

The facility will provide housekeeping and maintenance services.

The facility will assure you have clean bath and bed linens and that they are in good repair.

The facility will provide you with private closet space as space permits.

The facility will provide you with adequate and comfortable lighting and sound levels.

The facility will provide you with comfortable and safe temperature levels.

–Appendix F–

NURSING HOME CHECKLIST

Nursing Home Checklist from ***www.Medicare.gov***

Checklists can help you evaluate the nursing homes that you call or visit. Use a new checklist for each home you call or visit. (Copy from this book or print from the Medicare Website.) Then, compare the scores. This will help you select a nursing home that is a good choice for you or your relative.

Nursing Home Name:

____

Date Visited:

____

Address:

____

Basic Information

Is the facility Medicare certified?

____(yes) _____(no)

Is the facility Medicaid certified?

____(yes) _____(no)

Is this a skilled nursing facility?

____(yes) _____(no)

Is the facility accepting new patients?

____(yes) _____(no)

Is there a waiting period for admission?

____(yes) _____(no)

Is a skilled bed available to you?

____(yes) _____(no)

Useful Tips

Generally, skilled nursing care is available only for a short period of time after a hospitalization. Custodial care is for a much longer period of time. If a facility offers both types of care, learn if residents may transfer between levels of care within the nursing home without having to move from their old room or from the nursing home. Nursing homes that only take Medicaid residents might offer longer term but less intensive levels of care. Nursing Homes that don't accept Medicaid payment may make a resident move when Medicare or the resident's own money runs out.

An occupancy rate is the total number of residents currently living in a nursing home divided by the home's total number of beds. Occupancy rates vary by area, depending on the overall number of available nursing home beds.

Nursing Home Information:

Is the home and the current administrator licensed?

____(yes) _____(no)

Does the home conduct background checks on all staff?

____(yes) _____(no)

Does the home have special services units?

____(yes) _____(no)

Does the home have abuse prevention training?

____(yes) _____(no)

Useful Tips

- LICENSURE: The nursing home and its administrator should be licensed by the State to operate.
- BACKGROUND CHECKS: Do the nursing home's procedures to screen potential employees for a history of abuse meet your State's requirements? Your State's Ombudsman program might be able to help you with this information.
- SPECIAL SERVICES: Some nursing homes have special service units like rehabilitation, Alzheimer's, and hospice. Learn if there are separate waiting periods or facility guidelines for when residents would be moved on or off the special unit.
- STAFF TRAINING: Do the nursing home's training programs educate employees about how to recognize resident abuse and neglect, how to deal with aggressive or difficult residents, and how to deal with the stress of caring for so many needs? Are there clear procedures to identify events or trends that might lead to abuse and neglect, and on how to investigate, report, and resolve your complaints?
- LOSS PREVENTION: Are there policies or procedures to safeguard resident possessions?

For Sections III through VI, give the nursing home a grade from one to five. One is worst, five is best.

Quality of Life:

Worst Best

1 2 3 4 5 1. Residents can make choices about their daily routine. Examples are when to go to bed or get up, when to bathe, or when to eat.

1 2 3 4 5 2. The interaction between staff and patient is warm and respectful.

1 2 3 4 5 3. The home is easy to visit for friends and family.

1 2 3 4 5 4. The nursing home meets your cultural, religious, or language needs.

1 2 3 4 5 5. The nursing home smells and looks clean and has good lighting.

1 2 3 4 5 6. The home maintains comfortable temperatures.

1 2 3 4 5 7. The resident rooms have personal articles and furniture.

1 2 3 4 5 8. The public and resident rooms have comfortable furniture.

1 2 3 4 5 9. The nursing home and its dining room are generally quiet.

1 2 3 4 5 10. Residents may choose from a variety of activities that they like.

1 2 3 4 5 11. The nursing home has outside volunteer groups.

1 2 3 4 5 12. The nursing home has outdoor areas for resident use and helps residents to get outside.

TOTAL: ____________ (Best Possible Score: 60)

Quality of Care:

Worst Best

1 2 3 4 5 1. The facility corrected any Quality of Care deficiencies that were in the State inspection report.

1 2 3 4 5 2. Residents may continue to see their personal physician.

1 2 3 4 5 3. Residents are clean, appropriately dressed, and well groomed.

1 2 3 4 5 4. Nursing Home staff respond quickly to requests for help.

1 2 3 4 5 5. The administrator and staff seem comfortable with each other and with the residents.

1 2 3 4 5 6. Residents have the same care givers on a daily basis.

1 2 3 4 5 7. There are enough staff at night and on week-ends or holidays to care for each resident.

1 2 3 4 5 8. The home has an arrangement for emergency situations with a nearby hospital.

1 2 3 4 5 9. The family and residents councils are independent from the nursing home's management.

1 2 3 4 5 10. Care plan meetings are held at times that are easy for residents and their family members to attend.

TOTAL:____________ (Best Possible Score: 50)

Useful Tips

Good care plans are essential to good care. They should be put together by a team of providers and family and updated as often as necessary.

Nutrition and Hydration (Diet and Fluids):

Worst Best

1 2 3 4 5 1. The home corrected any deficiencies in these areas that were on the recent state inspection report.

1 2 3 4 5 2. There are enough staff to assist each resident who requires help with eating.

1 2 3 4 5 3. The food smells and looks good and is served at proper temperatures.

1 2 3 4 5 4. Residents are offered choices of food at mealtimes.

1 2 3 4 5 5. Residents' weight is routinely monitored.

1 2 3 4 5 6. There are water pitchers and glasses on tables in the rooms.

1 2 3 4 5 7. Staff help residents drink if they are not able to do so on their own.

1 2 3 4 5 8. Nutritious snacks are available during the day and evening.

1 2 3 4 5 9. The environment in the dining room encourages residents to relax, socialize, and enjoy their food.

TOTAL: ____________ (Best Possible Score: 45)

Useful Tips

Ask the professional staff how the medicine a resident takes can affect what they eat and how often they may want something to drink.

Visit at mealtime. Are residents rushed through meals or do they have time to finish eating and to use the meal as an opportunity to socialize with each other?

Sometimes the food a home serves is fine, but a resident still won't eat. Nursing home residents may like some control over their diet. Can they select their meals from a menu or select their mealtime?

If residents need help eating, do care plans specify what type of assistance they will receive?

Safety

Worst Best

1 2 3 4 5 1. There are handrails in the hallways and grab bars in the bathrooms.

1 2 3 4 5 2. Exits are clearly marked.

1 2 3 4 5 3. Spills and other accidents are cleaned up quickly.

1 2 3 4 5 4. Hallways are free of clutter and have good lighting.

1 2 3 4 5 5. There are enough staff to help move residents quickly in an emergency.

1 2 3 4 5 6. The nursing home has smoke detectors and sprinklers.

TOTAL: ____________ (Best Possible Score: 30)

Useful Tips Relating to Information in Nursing Home Compare

Nursing Home Compare contains summary information about nursing homes from their last state inspection. It also contains information that was reported by the nursing homes prior to the last State inspection including nursing home and resident characteristics. If you have questions or concerns about the information on a nursing home, you should discuss them during your visit. This section contains useful tips and questions that you may want to ask the nursing home staff, family members and residents of the nursing home during your visit.

Nursing Home Compare Information on Results of Nursing Home Inspections

Bring a copy of the Nursing Home Compare inspection results for the nursing home. Ask whether the deficiencies have been corrected. Ask to see a copy of the most recent nursing home inspection report.

Nursing Home Compare Information on Resident and Nursing Home Characteristics

For the Measure: Residents with Physical Restraints

Does it appear that there is sufficient staff to assist residents who need help in moving or getting in and out of chairs and bed?

Ask the Director of Nursing who is involved in the decisions about physical restraints.

When physical restraints are used, do the staff remove the physical restraints on a regular basis to help residents with moving, and with activities of daily living?

Do the staff help residents with physical restraints to get in and out of bed and chairs when they want to get up?

Do staff help residents with physical restraints to move as much as they would like to?

For the Measure: Residents with Pressure (Bed) Sores

Ask the staff how they identify if a resident is at risk for skin breakdown. Ask them what they do to prevent pressure sores for these residents.

Ask the staff about the percentage of their residents that have pressure sores and why.

Do you see staff helping residents change their positions in wheelchairs, chairs, and beds?

For the Measure: Residents with Bowel and Bladder Incontinence

Does the nursing home smell clean?

Ask the staff what steps they take to prevent bowel and bladder incontinence for residents who are at risk.

For the Measure: Residents Who Are Very Dependent in Eating

Look at your response to Question 2 in Section V above.

Observe residents who need help in eating. Are they able to finish their meals or is the food returned to the kitchen uneaten?

For the Measure: Residents Who Are Bedfast

Ask the Director of Nursing how staff are assigned to care for these residents.

For the Measure: Residents With Restricted Joint Motion

Ask the Director of Nursing how the nursing home cares for residents with restricted joint motion.

Do the residents get help with getting out of chairs and beds when they want to get up?

For the Measure: Residents with Unplanned Weight Gain or Loss

Look at your responses to Questions 2, 3, 4, 5, 8, and 9 in section V above.

For the Measure: Residents with Behavioral Symptoms

What management and/or medical approaches for behavioral symptoms are being used by the nursing home?

How does staff handle residents that have behavioral symptoms such as calling out or yelling?

Ask whether residents with behavioral symptoms are checked by a doctor or behavioral specialist.

Ask whether staff get special training to help them to provide care to residents with behavioral symptoms.

Nursing Home Compare Information on Nursing Staff

Caring, competent nursing staff who respect each resident and family member are very important in assuring that residents get needed care and enjoy the best possible quality of life. Adequate nursing staff is needed to assess resident needs, plan and give them care, and help them with eating, bathing and other activities. Some residents (e.g., those who are more dependent in eating or who are bedfast) need more help than other residents depending on their conditions. The combinations of registered nurses (RNs), licensed practical and vocational nurses (LPNs/LVNs), and certified nursing assistants (CNAs)that nursing homes may have vary depending on the type of care that residents need and the number of residents in the nursing home.

Look at your responses to Questions 2 and 5 in section III above and Questions 4, 5, and 10 in section IV above. Also look at your responses to Questions 2 and 7 in section V above.

Are nursing staff members courteous and friendly to residents and to other staff?

Do nursing staff respond timely to residents calls for assistance such as help getting in and out of bed, dressing and going to the bathroom?

Observe meal times. Do all residents who need assistance with eating get help? Do staff give each resident enough time to chew food thoroughly and complete the meal?

Which nursing staff members are involved in planning the residents individual care? (Are they the same ones who give the care to residents?)

Ask questions about staff turnover. Is there frequent turnover among certified nursing assistants (CNAs)? What about nurses and supervisors, including the Director of Nursing and the Administrator? If staff changes frequently, ask why.

While the number of nursing staff is important to good care, also consider other factors, such as education and training. How many registered nurses (RNs) are on the staff, and how many available on each shift? What kind of training do certified nursing assistants (CNAs) receive? How does the nursing home ensure that all staff receive continuing education and keep their knowledge and skills up-to-date?

–Appendix G–

FORMS

MEDICAL AUTHORIZATION

I ____, parent of
____, authorize
____ (grandparent)
to obtain health care for my child ___________________________
and make medical decisions in my absence. This includes all emergency and nonemergency health care, dental care, vision care, and any other health care.

____

notarized:___________________________________

Permission to Release Medical Information

To: Dr. ___________________________

I, ____________________________________ (parent's name), request that ________________________________ (caretaker's name), my son/daughter/_________________(other relationship), be given full access to all of my medical records maintained by your office, now and in the future. I request that all medical and office personnel speak freely with ___________________ (caretaker's name) about my health and medical information.

Check if applicable:

_______ I request that this office contact ___________________ (caretaker) directly by phone (at the following number _____________________________) instead of me with test results, appointment information and all other telephone communication. I also request that all written correspondence be directed to him or her at the following address: __________________________________

OR

_______ I request that this office contact ___________________ (caretaker) as well as me by phone (at the following number: _____________________________) with test results, appointment information and all other telephone communication. I also request that all written correspondence be copied to him or her at this address: ____.

_____________________________ ____________

Signature Date

Basic Information Organization Sheet

I. GENERAL INFORMATION

Name: ____

Name at birth if different: ___________________________

Address: ____

____

Phone Number: _______________________________________

Previous Addresses: ___________________________________

____

Social Security Number: ________________________________

Date of Birth: ____

II. HEALTH INSURANCE

Medicare number: ____________________________________

Medicaid number: ____________________________________

Other health insurance (list number, group number, company and type of insurance):

____

____

____

II. INCOME INFORMATION

Monthly Social Security Income:__________________________

Pension income: _____________________________________

Veteran's income:_____________________________________

Other income:____

Source: ____

III. REAL ESTATE

(a) Primary residence:: ______________________________

value: ______________________________

Equity: ____________ Mortgage amount: ____________

Bank: ______________________________

Names on account: ______________________________

(b) Other residences or property: ______________________________

value: ______________________________

Equity: ____________ Mortgage amount: ____________

Bank: ______________________________

Names on account: ______________________________

(c) Other residences or property: ______________________________

value: ______________________________

Equity: ____________ Mortgage amount: ____________

Bank: ______________________________

Names on account: ______________________________

IV. BANKS

(a) Savings Account number: ____________ Bank: ____________

Current balance: ______________________________

Names on account: ______________________________

(b) Checking Account number: ____________ Bank: ____________

Current balance: ______________________________

Names on Account: ______________________________

(c) Other bank account number: ____________ Bank: ____________

current balance: ______________________________

Names on account: ______________________________

(d) Other bank account number:__________ Bank:________________

Current balance: ____

Names on account: ______________________________________

(e) CD Account number:___________ Bank: ____________________

Current balance: ____

Names on account: ______________________________________

(f) CD Account number:___________ Bank:_____________________

Current balance: ____

Names on account: ______________________________________

V. INVESTMENTS

(a) Account number: _______________________________________

Name of institution, fund or stock: _________________________

Current balance: ____

Names on Account: _______________________________________

(b) Account number: _______________________________________

Name of institution, fund or stock _________________________

Current balance: ____

Names on Account: _______________________________________

VI. INSURANCE

(a) Life insurance policy number: _____________________________

Company: ____

Face value:____________ beneficiary: ______________________

(b) Life insurance policy number: _____________________________

Company: ____

Face value:____________ beneficiary: ______________________

(c) Homeowner's or renter's insurance policy number: ___________

Company: ____

Property insured: ____

VII. VEHICLES

(a) Type of Vehicle:________________ Year: ____________________

Approximate value:_____________ Name on title: ___________

Insurance policy number:__________ Company:_____________

(b) Type of Vehicle:________________ Year: ____________________

Approximate value:_____________ Name on title: ___________

Insurance policy number:__________ Company:_____________

VIII. PERSONAL PROPERTY

(a) Safety Deposit Box Number: _______________________________

Location ________________ Contents:______________________

Location of key or password: _______________________________

(b) Safety Deposit Box Number: _______________________________

Location________________ Contents: ______________________

Location of key or password: _______________________________

(c) Important or valuable item of property:_____________________

value:____________ Location: _____________________________

(d) Important or valuable item of property:_____________________

value:____________ Location: _____________________________

(e) Important or valuable item of property:_____________________

value:____________ Location: _____________________________

(f) Important or valuable item of property:_____________________

value:____________ Location: _____________________________

IX. OTHER ASSETS

Please list all other assets of value or importance, including interest in a business, loans owned, investment property, and any other asset or property not previously listed. Specify the location of the item and value.

____

____

____

____

____

____

____

____

____

____

____

____

____

INDEX

D

E

F

G

H

I

J

L

M

N

S

T

U

V

W

ABOUT THE AUTHOR

Brette McWhorter Sember received her J.D. from the State University of New York at Buffalo. She practiced law in New York state and was a member of the Surrogate's Court committee of the Bar Association of Erie County. She was on the Guardian ad litem panel in two counties. Her practice included estate planning and probate.

Sember is experienced in helping seniors sort through options and evaluate choices that involve lifestyle, care facilities, finances and estate and health planning. Her one to one experience with seniors gave her understanding about the deeply personal nature of senior planning and also developed her belief that senior planning is an issue for the entire family. Additionally, her own family experience with aging grandparents makes senior care a day to day issue.

Sember is the author of several self-help legal guides that deal with family and financial issues. She writes and speaks often about law.

Visit her web site at **www.MooseintheBirdbath.com**